Plain English
Real Estate Dictionary

2nd Edition
Marlyss A. Bird

Allied Business Schools, Inc.

This publication is designed to provide accurate and current information regarding the subject matter covered. The principles and conclusions presented are subject to local, state and federal lows and regulations, court cases, and revisions of same. If legal advice or other expert assistance is required, the reader is urged to consult a competent professional in that field.

Director of Publishing: *Lars Jentsch*
Real Estate Publisher: *Leigh Conway*
Editor: *Sue Carlson*

Ashley Crown Systems, Inc.
22952 Alcalde Drive
Laguna Hills, CA 92653

Printed in the United States of America
ISBN 0-934772-72-X

10-01-06

Introduction

The goal in creating the Plain English Real Estate Dictionary was to define the concepts of the real estate profession for real estate students and others.

Allied Business Schools, Inc. is always looking for ways to clarify real estate concepts and make them more understandable.

In addition to clear and concise definitions, this book includes charts showing the connections between related terms, real estate math, and measurement conversion tables.

Allied Business Schools, Inc. believes that these definitions will help all real estate students to understand and appreciate more completely the real estate profession.

About the Author

Marlyss Bird has written, edited, and designed educational materials for several Allied Business School real estate and appraisal courses.

Marlyss holds a Bachelor's degree in Journalism and French from the University of Oregon. She also has worked in the real estate industry in several capacities, including REALTOR's® assistant and commercial real estate assistant.

Table of Contents

A

abandonment
The act of voluntarily surrendering or relinquishing possession of real property without transferring title to someone else. Non-use of the property does not prove abandonment.

abatement
A reduction or decrease; usually applies to rent or taxes.

able
Financial ability, as in "ready, willing, and able buyer."

abnormal sale
An appraisal term referring to a sale of real property that is unusual for its particular marketplace. For example, a parent sells a piece of property to their child at a price lower than market value. An appraiser must be careful when considering use of an abnormal sale as a comparable.

absentee owner
A property owner who does not live on the property and may rely on a property manager to oversee it.

absolute
Without limitations, restrictions or conditions.

absorption bed
A shallow trench containing a pipe that carries effluent away from the septic tank into an open area, where it is absorbed into the soil.

absorption rate
The rate at which vacant space (commercial or residential) is either leased or sold; usually expressed in square feet per year or number of units per year.

abstraction
An appraisal method of calculating land value. The value is achieved by deducting all improvement costs (less depreciation) from the sales price. Also called extraction or allocation.

abstract of judgment
A document used to execute a judgment lien. It must be filed in all counties where the judgment debtor owns real estate.

abstract of title
A historical summary of a piece of land, compiled from public records or documents. The abstract includes all grants, conveyances, wills, records, and judicial proceedings affecting the title. It is useful for showing continuity of ownership and any other elements of record that may impair title.

abstractor
A person who researches anything affecting the title to real property and summarizes the resulting information in a report called an abstract of title.

abut
To touch, border on, or be contiguous to.

abutting property
Property that touches or is contiguous to another property, as opposed to being near or adjacent to another property.

acceleration clause
A clause in a loan document describing certain events that would cause the entire loan to be due. Possible events include sale of the property, or failure to repay the debt.

acceptance
An unqualified agreement to the terms of an offer.

accessibility
The ease of entrance and exit of a property. Accessibility is a factor in determining the most profitable use of a property.

accession
The acquisition of additional property through the efforts of man, such as improvements, or by natural forces, such as alluvial deposits.

access to property
A requirement of the seller in a transaction. The seller must provide reasonable access to the property to: the buyer, inspectors representing the buyer, and representatives of lending institutions for appraisal purposes or for any other purpose relating to the sale.

accommodation party
A person who helps another to secure credit by signing a note or other obligation without receiving consideration in return.

accommodation recording
The process of a title company recording instruments, or papers, with the county recorder. This is performed as a convenience to a customer, and the information is not guaranteed correct or valid.

Accredited Management Organization (AMO)
A property management designation offered by the Institute of Real Estate Management (IREM) to property management companies that meet prescribed high standards.

Accredited Residential Manager (ARM)
A property management designation offered by the Institute of Real Estate Management (IREM). Requirements for designation include management experience, additional training, and adherence to a code of ethics.

accretion
A buildup of soil by natural causes on property bordering a river, lake, or ocean.

accrue
To accumulate, grow, or mature over a period of time; as in accrued interest on a loan.

accrued depreciation
The difference between the cost of replacement or reproduction, and the current appraised value of a property.

acknowledgment
A statement made in front of a notary public, or other person who is authorized to administer oaths, stating that a document bearing your signature was actually signed by you.

ACM (asbestos containing material)
Asbestos combined with other materials. The resulting substance can be more dangerous than asbestos alone, as it can easily flake or crumble and be ingested or inhaled.

Acquired Immunodeficiency Syndrome (AIDS)
An incurable disease that attacks an individual's immune system. Persons who are afflicted with this disease are protected under most federal and state housing anti-discrimination laws.

acquisition appraisal
An appraisal that estimates the market value of a property facing condemnation under the government's powers of eminent domain. The appraisal is performed to determine the amount of just compensation due to the owner.

acquisition cost
The cost of acquiring property in addition to the purchase price. Cost includes escrow fees, title insurance, lenders fees, etc.

acre
A piece of land measuring 43,560 square feet.

acre foot
A volume of material such as water, sand, coal, etc., equal to an area of one acre with a depth of one foot. If a liquid, equal to 325,850 gallons.

acreage
A large piece of property that is usually unimproved. Acreage may be used for agricultural, industrial, residential or commercial uses.

acreage zoning
Zoning that reduces residential density by requiring large building lots. Also called large-lot zoning or snob zoning.

action
A lawsuit brought to court.

action price
The price of a piece of real property that is lower than the asking price and that will generate more interest from potential buyers, and serious negotiations toward a sale.

act of God
An act attributable to nature without human interference. Such acts include tidal wave, flood, hurricane, volcanic eruption, earthquake, and fire. The occurrence of an act of God may temporarily or permanently relieve parties in an agreement of their responsibilities.

actual age
The chronological, real age of a building. It is the opposite of its effective age, which is determined by the building's condition and utility.

actual cash value
The monetary worth of an improvement. The cost of replacing the improvement, less any depreciation.

actual damages
Damages that a court of law recognizes as the result of a wrong.

actual depreciation
Depreciation occurring as a result of physical, functional or economic forces, causing loss in value to a building.

actual notice
Knowledge that is based on things actually seen, heard, read or observed. Notice may also be given by possession of property. As opposed to constructive notice.

ADA (Americans with Disabilities Act)
A federal law designed to eliminate discrimination against individuals with disabilities by mandating equal access to jobs, public accommodations, government services, public transportation, and telecommunications.

ADAAG (Americans with Disabilities Act Accessibility Guidelines)
A document that provides standards to be observed in the design, construction, and alteration of buildings that come under the jurisdiction of the ADA.

ad valorem
A Latin phrase meaning "according to value." It is usually used in connection with real estate taxation. Local governments levy real property taxes based on the assessed value; therefore property taxes are known as ad valorem taxes.

add-on rate
A method of computing interest. The interest is charged on the entire principal amount for the specified term, regardless of any periodic repayments of principal that are made.

addendum
An addition or change to a contract; a supplement. All addendums to an agreement should be dated and signed or initialed by all parties involved.

additional deposit
Additional earnest money given in a purchase agreement. Often requested by the buyer's agent when a number of offers are expected on the property, and the agent wants the seller to know that her client is very serious about the offer. Additional deposit is also used if the buyer can only make a small initial earnest money deposit. The broker should seek an additional deposit soon after acceptance of the offer, to bring the total earnest money amount to 5 or 10 percent of the purchase price. It is important to collect the earnest money as it covers the costs of the transaction in case the buyer defaults.

additional interest due/payoffs

An agreement between the buyer and seller that the lender must receive any payoff for encumbrances due at the close of escrow by a specific date in order to avoid additional accrued interest. If the lender requires additional funds after the close of escrow, the buyer and seller must deposit those funds into the appropriate accounts.

add-on interest

Interest charged to, and paid by, the borrower that is computed on the full principal amount for the entire loan period term, regardless of how much principal is repaid. Also called block interest.

Adjustable Rate Mortgage (ARM)

A loan whose interest rate is periodically adjusted to more closely coincide with current interest rates. The adjustment amounts and times are agreed upon when the loan is created.

adjusted cost basis

The original purchase price of a property, plus any capital improvements and any costs of the sale, less depreciation. Also called adjusted book basis.

adjusted sales price

The estimated sales price of a comparable property after adjustments have been made to compensate for differences between the subject property and the comparable. The price the comparable property would sell for if it possessed all the characteristics of the subject property.

adjustments

An appraisal term used when comparing properties in order to assess value. If a comparable property has a certain feature that the subject property does not have, or lacks a feature the subject property does have, the assessed value is adjusted accordingly. The increases or decreases in the value are the adjustments. Also, when referring to real estate closings, adjustments are the credits and debits listed on a settlement statement.

administered price system
The procedure used by FNMA to purchase mortgages. Beginning in 1983, FNMA, or Fannie Mae, changed from a free-market-system auction to the administered price system. Instead of buying the lowest-priced loans, or those with the deepest discounts as before, FNMA now adjusts its required yields daily to reflect changing market factors and FNMA's financial needs.

administrative assistant
A person who assists any of the executive or middle management personnel in the achievement of their job objectives.

administrator
A person appointed by the court to handle the affairs of a deceased person when there is no one mentioned in a will to do so.

adobe construction
A structure built of adobe blocks. Adobe is mud mixed with straw and then baked. A very good, but expensive building material.

advance
Payments made by the lender to a delinquent borrower to cover such charges as taxes, insurance, and foreclosure costs. The advance may be made to prevent a foreclosure.

advance fee
A fee paid before any services are rendered. Some brokers obtain a nonrefundable advance fee from the seller, to cover the costs of advertising the listed property. This practice is sometimes considered improper.

adverse land use
A form of land use that causes the value of surrounding land to decrease. An example of adverse land use is an industrial park in a residential area.

adverse possession
A method of acquiring title to property by continued possession and payment of taxes, rather than by purchase or conveyance. Similar to prescription; however, prescription results in only a limited interest in the property and does not require the payment of taxes.

adverse use
The access and use of property without the owner's consent, such as a pathway across another's property.

advertising
Publicly promoting one's products or services. In real estate, a broker must have written permission from the seller to advertise their property.

aesthetic value
The value of a property due to features of the property that are exceptionally attractive or pleasing. Aesthetic value may be protected by zoning ordinances or building codes.

AFIDA (Agricultural Foreign Investment Disclosure Act)
A law passed in 1978 that requires foreigners who have an interest in U.S. agricultural land that exceeds one acre to file disclosure information with the Secretary of Agriculture.

affidavit
A written statement or declaration made under oath before a licensed individual, such as a notary public.

affidavit of title (affidavit of ownership)
A written statement, made under oath by a seller or grantor of real property and acknowledged by a notary public, in which the grantor identifies himself or herself and indicates marital status, certifies that no defects have occurred in the title since the examination of the title on the date of the contracts, and certifies that he or she is in possession of the property (if applicable).

affinity
Not related by blood; related by marriage.

affirmation
An alternative to an oath, which can be used by people whose religious beliefs will not allow an oath.

affordable housing
Housing for individuals or families who are considered low-income by HUD (U.S. Department of Housing and Urban Development). Affordable housing projects are usually developed with governmental assistance.

a-frame construction
A style of residential construction that has steeply-sloped roofs, and resembles the letter A.

after acquired title
Title that is acquired after a property has been conveyed. For example, Bob conveys his property to Al, but it is discovered that Bob does not hold a valid title to the property. When the title is eventually made valid, Al will automatically acquire good title to the property.

after-tax cash flow (ATCF)
The cash flow remaining from the net operating income after paying income taxes, debt service, and loan repayments.

age
The chronological lifespan of a person or object. A consideration when determining legal capacity to enter into contracts, also a feature of anti-discrimination housing laws. A person must be of the age of majority to legally enter into valid contracts. The age of majority is set by state laws and may differ between states. Some states prohibit housing discrimination based on age, although federal housing laws do not yet cover age.

age-life depreciation
An appraisal method of computing accrued depreciation. It assumes that a building depreciates at a fixed rate over the course of its life. The depreciation is then calculated by dividing the total economic life by its current effective age. Also called the straight-line method.

agency
A relationship in which one party (principal) authorizes another party (agent) to act as the principal's representative in dealing with third parties.

agency by estoppel
An agency relationship between a broker and a principal that is created when a principal causes a third party to believe that the agency exists by words or actions. If the third party then deals with the supposed agent, the principal is estopped, or prevented, from denying the agency relationship, because of his or her earlier words or deeds.

agency by ratification
An agency relationship created when the agent act as if an agency relationship exists, before an official agreement or contract is expressed. The principal agrees to the relationship after the act is performed, thereby ratifying the act and the agency relationship.

agency relationship confirmation
A disclosure statement confirming the agency relationship that exists in a particular transaction. The statement reflects that the selling agent may work for either the buyer or seller exclusively, or both at once.

agency securities
Low-risk debt obligations issued by government agencies such as Fannie Mae and Freddie Mac. Agency securities are similar to U.S. Treasury Bills in that they pay interest and have low default risk. However, the main differences are that they are not backed entirely by the U.S. Government and the interest income is taxed differently.

agent
Anyone who has the authority to act on the behalf of another, representing the business interests of that person.

aggregate deductible
The deductible in some property insurance contracts that is assessed on an annual aggregate, or cumulative, basis rather than on a per claim basis. In this arrangement, the insured pays a fixed amount, and the insurance provider pays the rest, when that aggregate deductible amount is exceeded.

agrarian
Relating to land.

agreement of sale
A contract for the sale of real property in which the seller gives up possession, but retains title until the purchase price is paid in full.

Agricultural Foreign Investment Disclosure Act (AFIDA)
A law passed in 1978 that requires foreigners who have an interest in U.S. agricultural land that exceeds one acre to file disclosure information with the Secretary of Agriculture.

agricultural land
Land used for farming purposes, including growing crops and raising livestock.

agricultural lien
A lien taken out by a farmer to obtain money or supplies for farming activities. The lien is attached only to the crop, not to the land.

AH&MA (American Hotel and Motel Association)
The lodging industry's trade association. The association provides assistance in operations, education, and communications, and lobbies the government on behalf of the lodging industry.

AHERA (Asbestos Hazard Emergency Response Act)
A law passed by Congress in 1986 that amends the Toxic Substances Control Act (TSCA). It requires all public schools to be inspected for the presence of asbestos and to remedy the problem if it is likely to be hazardous to people's health.

AIDA Formula
In marketing, a formula for writing an ad that is designed to get maximum results: A=Attention, I=Interest, D=Desire, A=Action.

AIDS (Acquired Immunodeficiency Syndrome)
An incurable disease that attacks an individual's immune system. Persons who are afflicted with this disease are protected under most federal and state housing anti-discrimination laws.

airport zoning
Zoning regulations in and around airports that restrict building height and natural growth, in order to minimize potential hazards to aircraft.

air rights
Property rights that extend to an indefinite distance upward from the land.

airport hotel
A lodging accommodation to meet travelers' needs at the beginning or end of a journey. Airport hotels are located at or near an airport. Modern hotels of this type include conference rooms, fitness centers, and restaurants.

AITD (all-inclusive trust deed)
A method of financing in which a new junior loan is created that includes both the unpaid principal balance of the first loan and whatever new sums are loaned by the lender. Interest is charged on the overall total of the AITD, invariably at a higher rate than that charged on the included trust deeds. Also called a wrap-around mortgage.

alcove
A recessed part or addition to a room.

ALDA (American Land Development Association)
A national trade association of the real estate development industry. Membership includes professionals primarily involved with recreational and second homes.

aleatory contract
A contract that depends on a contingency or an uncertain future event, or where the monetary values of the parties' performance are unequal. An insurance policy is an aleatory contract because the insurer's obligation to pay a loss depends on uncertain events, while the insured must pay a fixed premium during the policy period.

alien
A person not born in the United States, and who has not been naturalized and is not a citizen. In most states, aliens are allowed to acquire and hold an interest in land, with some limitations.

alienate
To transfer ownership or sell a property.

alienation clause
A clause in a contract giving the lender certain rights in the event of the sale or other transfer of a mortgaged property.

all-inclusive trust deed (AITD)
A method of seller financing often used with commercial property. The all-inclusive trust deed secures a wrap-around loan that incorporates both the unpaid principal balance of the first loan and whatever new sums are loaned by the lender. The existing mortgages stay on the property and the new mortgage wraps around them. Interest is charged on the overall total of the AITD, invariably at a higher rate than that charged on the included trust deeds. Also called a wrap-around mortgage.

allocation
An appraisal method of calculating land value. The value is achieved by deducting all improvement costs (less depreciation) from the sales price. Also called extraction or abstraction.

allodial system
Our modern system of free and full land ownership by individuals, as opposed to the feudal system in which land ownership was vested in the king and represented only the right to use the land.

all-suite hotel
A hotel offering full suites to its guests similar to one-bedroom apartments. Traveling business people who are in one area for several days or weeks at a time often uses these hotels.

alluvial deposit
Sand or mud, carried by water and deposited on land.

alluvium
Soil that builds up as a result of accretion.

ALTA (American Land Title Association)
An association of land title companies that promotes the safe and efficient transfer of ownership and interest in real property, provides information to consumers, and maintains professional standards and ethics.

ALTA Policy
American Land Title Association policy of extended title insurance. The policy protects against all standard risks, plus other unrecorded risks such as mechanic's liens, physical easements, and some water claims. The policy is designed to protect lenders, but can be purchased by the lender or buyer.

alterations
Changes made to the interior or exterior of a building that do not change its exterior dimensions.

ambulatory
Movable. When speaking of wills, it means revocable.

amending previous instructions
A clause in escrow instructions that gives new instructions that supersede and amend any previous instructions.

amenities
The qualities of a property, both tangible and intangible, that bring the owner satisfaction and non-monetary benefits. Examples are view, location, and recreational facilities.

American Hotel and Motel Association (AH&MA)
The lodging industry's trade association. The association provides assistance in operations, education, and communications, and lobbies the government on behalf of the lodging industry.

American bond
A style of bricklaying in which every 5th, 6th, or 7th layer of bricks is laid with the wide length facing the wall. All other layers have the narrow length facing the wall.

American Institute of Real Estate Appraisers (AIREA)
A professional organization that promotes professional practice and ethics in the real estate appraisal industry.

American Land Development Association (ALDA)
A national trade association of the real estate development industry. Membership includes professionals primarily involved with recreational and second homes.

American Land Title Association (ALTA)
An association of land title companies that promotes the safe and efficient transfer of ownership and interest in real property, provides information to consumers, and maintains professional standards and ethics.

American Society of Appraisers (ASA)
The oldest professional organization of appraisers. It promotes professional excellence through education, accreditation, publication, and other services. Members include personal property appraisers, business appraisers, and machine and jewelry appraisers in addition to real property appraisers.

American Society of Home Inspectors (ASHI)
A professional organization of home inspectors that builds public awareness of home inspection, and promotes excellence and exemplary practice.

Americans with Disabilities Act (ADA)
A federal law designed to eliminate discrimination against individuals with disabilities by mandating equal access to jobs, public accommodations, government services, public transportation, and telecommunications.

AMO (Accredited Management Organization)
A property management designation offered by the Institute of Real Estate Management (IREM) to property management companies that meet prescribed high standards.

amortization
The reduction of a debt through regular payments of both interest and principal.

amortization schedule
A schedule for payment of a mortgage, showing the amount of each payment, the payment number, interest payment, principal payment, total payment, and unpaid principal balance. Sometimes referred to as a curtail schedule.

amperage
The measurement of the strength of an electrical current.

Americans with Disabilities Act Accessibility Guidelines (ADAAG)
A document that provides standards to be observed in the design, construction, and alteration of buildings that come under the jurisdiction of the ADA.

anchor tenant
A major department or chain store located in a shopping center. The anchor tenant draws large numbers of consumers, generating maximum sales volume for the entire shopping center.

ancillary
Subordinate, supplementary, or auxiliary.

angle
The measurement in degrees between two intersecting lines.

annex
To add or attach. Usually to join a smaller or subordinate thing to a larger, more dominant thing. For example, a city can annex additional land to increase its size.

annual debt service
The total amount of all mortgage payments required in one year by a loan.

annual net income
The amount of income left from an income-producing property after all expenses have been deducted. Also called net operating income.

annual percentage rate (APR)
The cost of a mortgage stated as a yearly rate; includes such items as interest, mortgage insurance, and loan origination fee (points). Use of the APR permits a standard expression of credit costs, which facilitates easy comparison of lenders.

annuity
A series of equal or nearly equal payments made to an investor over a period of time. The rent due to a landlord under a lease is one example of an annuity.

antenuptial agreement
An agreement made between a man and woman before they wed, establishing property rights of each during the marriage, and in the event of their divorce or a death. Also called a prenuptial agreement.

anticipation, principle of
An appraisal principle that states that the current value of a property is affected by its perceived future value and/or benefit.

apostille
A certificate issued by the Secretary of State or other Notary regulating agency that proves the authenticity of a Notary's signature and seal. An apostille alone is sufficient proof of authentication for notarized documents exchanged between countries that abide by the Hague Convention; otherwise a chain of authenticating certificates may be necessary.

appeal
The act of requesting a higher law court to reconsider a decision made by a lower court, especially in order to reduce or prevent a punishment. Also, the request itself.

appliance
Non-industrial equipment such as dishwasher, electric range, air-conditioning, etc.

appointments
Equipment or furnishings used in the interior of a building, especially a home, which tend to increase comfort, appeal or utility.

appraisal

An estimate of the value of a property reached in a competent, objective, and impartial manner, using certain aspects of the property such as age, location, size, quality, etc. An opinion of value given by an appraiser.

Appraisal Foundation, The

A non-profit educational organization founded to create national appraisal standards and establish appraisal qualifications.

appraisal report

An appraiser's written opinion of a property's value, as of the date of appraisal.

Appraisal Standards Board (ASB)

An organization created by The Appraisal Foundation. The ASB establishes the rules for developing an appraisal and reporting its results. It is also responsible for the enforcement of USPAP (Uniform Standards of Professional Appraisal Practice).

appraised value

An opinion of value of a property at a specific time, based on facts such as location, improvements, age, etc.

appraiser

A person who is expected to perform a valuation service in a competent, objective, and impartial manner. Appraisers must be educated, trained, and licensed or certified.

Appraiser Qualifications Board (AQB)

An organization created by The Appraisal Foundation. The AQB establishes licensing and certifying standards and examination requirements for appraisers.

appreciation

An increase in value as a result of economic or other related changes. The increase may be temporary or permanent.

appurtenance

Any right, privilege or improvement that belongs to and transfers with property. Common appurtenances include rights-of-way, easements, water rights, and property improvements. Although they pass with the property, they are not necessarily part of the actual property.

APR (annual percentage rate)

The cost of a mortgage stated as a yearly rate; includes such items as interest, mortgage insurance, and loan origination fee (points). Use of the APR permits a standard expression of credit costs, which facilitates easy comparison of lenders.

AQB (Appraiser Qualifications Board)

An organization created by The Appraisal Foundation. The AQB establishes licensing and certifying standards and examination requirements for appraisers.

arbitrage

The buying and selling of money or securities in different markets for a profit. The term is most often used with regard to the difference in interest rates between wrap-around and underlying financing.

arbitration

A method of dispute resolution in which the claims are submitted to an objective third party. Arbitration is used to avoid going to court, and is frequently used to settle real estate disputes.

arch

A concave, curved span over a doorway, entire room, or building, such as an arched ceiling or roof.

arch rib roof

A roof usually used in industrial buildings that has the shape of an arch or crescent. It is supported by a bowstring truss that spreads the roof load evenly.

area
A piece of land. In a house, it refers to the entire expanse that makes up the structure, from basement to roof, from side to side.

armored cable
Two or more insulated wires enclosed in a metal sheathing.

arm's length transaction
A transaction between two unrelated or unaffiliated parties, so that there is no possibility of a conflict of interest. In this type of transaction, the property is fairly offered on the open market and both parties to the transaction act willingly and have full knowledge of the present condition of the property.

arrears
Refers to a payment that is made at the end of a time period. Also, a delinquency in paying a debt.

ASA (American Society of Appraisers)
The oldest professional organization of appraisers. It promotes professional excellence through education, accreditation, publication, and other services. Members include personal property appraisers, business appraisers, and machine and jewelry appraisers in addition to real property appraisers.

ASB (Appraisal Standards Board)
An organization created by The Appraisal Foundation. The ASB establishes the rules for developing an appraisal and reporting its results. It is also responsible for the enforcement of USPAP (Uniform Standards of Professional Appraisal Practice).

asbestos
Naturally occurring silicate minerals, which were formerly used for insulation and home products, but were found to be a health hazard and are no longer used.

asbestos containing material (ACMs)
Asbestos combined with other materials. The resulting substance can be more dangerous than asbestos alone, as it can easily flake or crumble and be ingested or inhaled.

Asbestos Hazard Emergency Response Act (AHERA)
A law passed by Congress in 1986 that amends the Toxic Substances Control Act (TSCA). It requires all public schools to be inspected for the presence of asbestos and to remedy the problem if it is likely to be hazardous to people's health.

ASHI (American Society of Home Inspectors)
A professional organization of home inspectors that builds public awareness of home inspection, and promotes excellence and exemplary practice.

ashlar
A stone that is cut in squares and used as a facing for masonry walls and in foundations.

"as-is"
Words in a contract that signify that the property is being purchased in its current state, and no guarantees are given regarding the subject property.

asking price
The price at which a piece of real estate is offered to the public.

asphalt
Smooth, hard, brittle black or brownish-black resinous mineral. Asphalt can also be made from products obtained in petroleum refining. It is commonly used for waterproofing and paving. The blackest asphalt is considered to be the best.

assemblage
The combining of several small adjoining properties to create one larger parcel under a single owner. Usually this is done to increase total value of all the properties involved.

assess
The act of determining a property's value for tax purposes.

assessed value
The appraised value of a piece of property, used in levying annual real estate taxes.

assessment
An estimate of property value used to determine property taxes, also the process of reaching the value estimate. An assessment may also be an additional tax used to raise money for a special purpose.

assessment base
The total value of all the assessed properties in a tax district or assessment district.

assessment district
An area that is under the authority of one assessor. It may consist of a single tax district or several.

assessment ratio
The assessed value of a property in comparison to its market value. Expressed as a fraction.

assessment roll
A list of all taxable property showing the assessed value of each parcel; it establishes the tax base. Also called a tax roll.

assessor
Someone who analyzes property and gives an opinion of its value for tax purposes.

asset
An item of value.

asset manager
In property management, an executive who works either for a large corporation or a professional property management firm, who oversees the company's real estate assets, and sets goals and strategies on behalf of the owners. Also called a portfolio manager.

assignee
The person to whom a claim, benefit, or right of property is transferred.

assignment
The transfer of a property's right, title, and interest from one person to another.

assignment of lease
The transfer of a tenant's title, right, and interest in real property.

assignment of rents
A lender's right to take possession and collect rents in the event of loan default.

assignor
The person transferring a claim, benefit, or right in property to another.

assistant manager (hotel)
The manager who relieves the general manager of selected duties, and interfaces with department heads.

association
A group of people who come together for business purposes. The group may be treated and taxed as a corporation by the IRS.

assumable mortgage
A mortgage that may be transferred to a third party without first obtaining approval from the lender.

assume
A term used in real estate transactions. The buyer may take over, or assume, responsibility for a pre-existing mortgage.

assumption clause
A clause in loan contracts that allows a buyer to take over the existing loan from the seller and become liable for repayment of the loan.

assumption of mortgage
The adoption by a buyer of an existing mortgage on a property he is purchasing. The buyer becomes personally liable for the terms and conditions of the mortgage, including the payments.

ATCF (after-tax cash flow)
The cash flow remaining from the net operating income after paying income taxes, debt service, and loan repayments.

attachment
The seizure of a defendant's property by court order in a lawsuit, and held as security for satisfaction of a judgment. The property may not be sold or otherwise freely encumbered until the attachment is removed.

attic
A room above the main living area, and just under the roof, of a house.

attorney fees
The amount of money an attorney charges for legal services rendered.

attorney in fact
A competent and disinterested person who is authorized by another person to act in his or her place in legal matters.

attornment
A tenant's acceptance of a new owner or landlord on the same property. Attornment often happens in long-term lease situations.

attractive nuisance
Any inherently dangerous object or condition that is likely to attract and harm children. A property owner is liable for injuries to a child due to such a hazard. For example, an unfenced swimming pool is an attractive nuisance.

auction
A usually public sale of goods or property, where people make successively higher offers of money for each item, until it is sold to the person who will pay the highest price. Real estate may be sold in this way, in the case of foreclosure sales, tax sales, and with hard-to-sell properties.

auctioneer
A person in charge of an auction who calls out the prices that people offer. Some states require real estate auctioneers to be licensed.

authorization to sell
A contract signed by a seller of property, authorizing an agent to obtain a potential buyer for the property. However, it does not authorize the agent to enter into a binding sales contract.

available funds
All the funds that are available to a borrower, or those that have been collected, including prepayments and advances given by the lender, or loan servicer.

avigation easement
An easement affecting land near airports. It allows aircraft to fly at low elevations over private property, and prevents property owners from making improvements or allowing trees to grow above a certain height. The extent of restriction depends on the glide angle required for safe landing and take-off.

avulsion
The sudden washing or tearing away of land by the action of water.

awning
A small canopy constructed of canvas, metal or other material that extends out over a window or doorway to protect from sun, rain, etc.

B

baby-boomers
The name given to the large number of people who were born in the years following World War II, from 1946 to 1964.

back-end ratio
The ratio of all fixed debt, including housing expenses, to gross income.

backfill
Material, usually earth, used to refill an excavated area. In home construction, backfill is used to fill in around foundation walls, to fill voids, or to compact loose soil.

back-of-the-house
Operations of the hotel business that prepare the hotel for guests and take place behind the scenes, out of the view of guests. Housekeeping is one example of a back-of-the-house function.

back-to-back escrow
An escrow agreement established by one party who is simultaneously selling a property and purchasing another.

back-to-back lease

An agreement by a landlord to take over a prospective tenant's existing lease in another property, in return for the tenant's commitment to lease space in the landlord's commercial property.

backup offer

A secondary offer. An offer to buy a property, submitted with the knowledge that a prior offer has already been submitted and accepted. The seller will often accept the backup offer, if the first offer fails.

balance sheet

A financial statement that reflects the current assets, liabilities, capital, and surplus of a business.

balanced trust

A type of real estate trust that combines real estate investment trusts and real estate mortgage trusts. The combination allows the beneficiaries to earn rental income, as well as mortgage interest and placement fees. Balanced trusts are called combination trusts outside of California.

balance, principle of

An appraisal principle that states that a property will realize its greatest value when the improvements are proportional to each other and to the property.

balance sheet

A report showing the assets, liabilities, and net worth of a business.

balcony

An open air platform extending outward from a building and enclosed by a railing.

balloon frame

A style of structure framing in which one-piece studs extend from the foundation to the roof and form the walls of both stories in a two-story structure.

balloon payment
A final loan payment that is substantially larger than the other payments and repays the debt in full.

balloon payment clause
A statement in escrow documents requiring the holder of the note to give the borrower at least 90 days, but not more than 150 days, notice before any balloon payment is due.

balloon payment disclosure
A clause in escrow documents, stating that all parties agree that they have not received or relied upon any statements made to them by the broker about the availability of funds or the rate of interest at the time the buyer must refinance or pay off the remaining balance of the loan.

balloon risk
The risk involved in assuming a loan with a balloon payment. A borrower may not be able to pay the required balloon payment at maturity.

Baltimore method
An appraisal method for determining the value of a corner lot using the value of inside lots. The corner lot is appraised for its frontage on both streets. For example, Corner Lot A fronts 100' on Bay Street and 100' on Oak Street. The value of a 100' inside lot on Bay Street is added to the value of a 100' inside lot on Oak Street to determine the value of Corner Lot A. Also called the Bernard Rule.

baluster
A vertical post that extends from the handrail to the bottom rail or stair on a staircase.

balustrade
A railing on a staircase that is made up of a handrail and balusters.

band of investment approach

A method of calculating the capitalization rate (rate of return on investment) of an income-producing property. It accounts for the different rates of return expected by the lender and the equity capital contributor. The word "band" refers to the bands of debt and equity capital required to support the investment.

The rate is calculated using the rate of return required by the lender (the mortgage constant) and the rate of return required by the equity investor (the equity capitalization rate). The method multiplies the percentage of the total value of the property contributed by each party, by the rate of return that each contributor demands, then adds the results. The number is the capitalization rate required to attract investors.

Example: Bob wants to buy a retail property for $500,000. The bank will loan $400,000 (80%). Bob will contribute $100,000 (20%). The bank expects a return of 8.8%. Bob expects a return of 10%. In order to meet their expectations, the property must return $45,000 total annually; $35,000 to the bank and $10,000 to Bob. The rate is 9%.

	Percent of Property's Total Value		Return Required		Rate
Lender	.80	x	.088	=	.07
Equity investor	.20	x	.10	=	.02
			Cap rate:		**.09**

Bank Insurance Fund (BIF)
In 1989, deposit insurance was consolidated under the Federal Deposit Insurance Corporation (FDIC). Two funds were established: the Bank Insurance Fund (BIF), which covers commercial banks and savings banks; and the Savings Association Insurance Fund (SAIF), which insures deposits at S&Ls. Insured banks, pay a premium on all their deposits.

banker's rule
A calendar standard by which prorations are calculated. When closing a real estate transaction, most escrow agents use a 360-day year (30 days in each month) to calculate prorations.

bankruptcy
A court proceeding to relieve a condition of financial insolvency (when a person's liabilities exceed their assets and the person is unable to pay current debts). Most or all of a person or company's debts are forgiven, at a loss to the creditors.

banquet director
In the lodging industry, the person in charge of all physical aspects of a banquet.

bargain sale
Property that is sold for less than its fair market value.

bargeboard
A decorative board that hangs from the projecting edge of a sloping roof. Commonly used in the 15th century. Also called a vergeboard.

base line
The major east-west line of the government or rectangular survey. This imaginary line intersects a principal meridian, and is used as a survey reference point.

basement
The area of a home or structure that is below ground level.

base rent
The minimum rent due in a percentage lease agreement.

baseboard
A finishing board affixed to the bottom of interior walls at the point where the base of the wall meets the floor.

baseboard heating
A heating system in which the baseboards of a house are replaced by the heating units.

basement
The floor of a building that is partially or completely underground.

basic activities
In economic base analysis, activities that produce goods intended for export. Basic activities may involve manufacturing, service or government.

basic industry
In economic base analysis, an industry that attracts income from outside the community.

basis
The value that the Internal Revenue Service assigns an asset. This is used as a point of reference to determine subsequent depreciation or appreciation of the asset.

basis point
Increments used to measure the change in interest rates. There are 100 basis points in one percent.

batten
Narrow strips of board used to hide joints between panels. In roofing, strips of wood used as the base for slate, clay tiles or wood shingles.

bay window
A window that projects in a curve out from a wall.

beam
A long thick piece of wood, metal or concrete, used to support weight in a building or other structure.

bearing wall
A wall supporting a floor or the roof of a building. In condominiums all bearing walls are common walls, shared by two or more units.

bed & breakfast inn
A lodging accommodation, generally converted from a large house or hotel, offering personal service to offer a pleasant get-away experience.

bedrock
Solid rock that is usually found a few feet beneath the topsoil. Bedrock is a good foundation support for structures.

before-and-after method
An appraisal technique used to determine the amount of compensation due to the owners of land that has been partially taken through condemnation. The value of the land before and after condemnation is calculated. The value of the remaining property is the difference between before and after condemnation.

before-tax cash flow (BTCF)
The portion of net operating income after debt service is paid, but before income tax is deducted. Also called equity dividend or pre-tax cash flow.

bell captain
The person in charge of the bellhops in the service department of a hotel.

bellhop
A service assistant in a hotel who ushers guests to their rooms, carries baggage, and offers other personal services.

belly-up
A slang term used to describe a failed business or real estate project, as in "the clothing store went belly-up."

belvedere
A small structure with a roof and open sides, usually in the garden, where one may sit and enjoy the view. Also called a gazebo.

beneficiary
The individual who benefits from a will, insurance policy, trust or other contract. Also the lender under a note and deed of trust.

beneficiary statement
A statement showing the status of a debt, including the unpaid balance of a loan.

benefit
The good or helpful effect of an improvement made to a previously private property, which was acquired under eminent domain.

bequest
A gift of personal property by will.

Bernard rule
An appraisal method for determining the value of a corner lot using the value of inside lots. The corner lot is appraised for its frontage on both streets. For example, Corner Lot A fronts 100' on Bay Street and 100' on Oak Street. The value of a 100' inside lot on Bay Street is added to the value of a 100' inside lot on Oak Street to determine the value of Corner Lot A. Also called the Baltimore method.

betterment
An improvement made to property that increases its value.

bid
An offer to purchase property for a certain amount. Or the act of submitting an offer to purchase something.

BIF (Bank Insurance Fund)
In 1989, deposit insurance was consolidated under the Federal Deposit Insurance Corporation (FDIC). Two funds were established: the Bank Insurance Fund (BIF), which covers commercial banks and savings banks; and the Savings Association Insurance Fund (SAIF), which insures deposits at S&Ls. Insured banks, pay a premium on all their deposits.

bilateral contract
A contract in which each party to the contract promises to perform some act or duty in exchange for the promise of the other party.

bill of sale
A written agreement used to transfer ownership in personal property.

bird dogging
Obtaining the initial lead regarding property, buyers, investors, potential home improvement customers, etc. The lead is then handed over to, and followed up by, someone else to make the deal.

bi-weekly payment loan
A loan that requires payment every two weeks, or twice a month. This results in an earlier loan repayment, and lower interest costs.

blanket mortgage
A loan secured by several properties. It is often used to secure construction financing.

blended rate
The interest rate of a newly refinanced loan. The interest rate is greater than the rate on the old loan, but is still less than the current market rate.

blighted area
A section of a city, generally the inner city, where a majority of the buildings are run-down, and property values are extremely low.

blockbusting
The illegal practice of causing panic selling by telling people that property values in a neighborhood will decline because of a specific event, such as the purchase of homes by minorities.

blue book
One of any number of real estate reference books that contain amortization and balloon payment tables.

blue-sky provision
A provision established by the Securities and Exchange Commission (SEC) that requires limited partnerships to disclose all risks involved in the investment. The provision was created in reaction to past misrepresentations and fraudulent profit claims.

board
The local chapter of the State Association of REALTORS®, which is part of the National Association of REALTORS®. Sometimes referred to as the state real estate commission.

board foot
A measurement of lumber equal to 12 inches by 12 inches by 1 inch, or 144 cubic inches.

board of REALTORS®
A local organization of licensed real estate brokers and salespersons. It is part of the National Association of REALTORS® and the State Association of REALTORS®.

boiler
A sealed tank in which water is turned into steam for heating or power.

bona fide
A Latin term meaning "in good faith." Actions that are in good faith and honest.

bona fide sale
The sale of property in a competitive market, at the current market price that represents good faith between the buyer and seller.

bond
An official document issued by a corporation or lender as evidence of a loan or mortgage.

bond rating
An assessment by financial reporting organizations of the relative financial risk of a issuing a bond.

book depreciation
An income tax term that refers to the calculation of constant depreciation or loss from the owner's original purchase price, or cost basis. The amount is taken as a tax deduction from the gross income. It may be used to offset other income, thus acting as a tax shelter, which is why many people purchase income property.

bookkeeper
In property management, the person who keeps the financial records of the properties under management.

book sale
A sale of real property to the state, in name only, when a taxpayer is delinquent in paying property taxes. The taxpayer does not actually lose title, retains possession, and has five years to pay the delinquent taxes. If the taxes are not paid within that five-year period a tax sale takes place, and the property may be sold at public auction to the highest bidder for cash.

book value
The initial value of the property plus additions and improvements, minus depreciation.

boot
Money or other property used to equalize the trade in a 1031 tax deferred exchange transaction if the value of one property is greater than the other.

borrower
A debtor; one who borrows money, in the form of a loan, and is obligated to repay it in full with interest.

boundaries
The perimeter or limit of a piece of land.

bounds
A directional reference, as in metes-and-bounds. Metes measure the length, and bounds limit the lengths to a certain area designated by monuments or landmarks.

BPI (buying power index)
A measure of demand in a certain area, relative to a given benchmark value. Common benchmarks are the United States and specific states or regions.

breach of contract
A failure to perform on part or all of the terms and conditions of a contract.

breakdown method
A method of calculating accrued depreciation by analyzing and measuring each cause of depreciation separately. The different types of depreciation are then added together to find the total depreciation.

break-even point
The point at which income is equal to costs.

breezeway
A canopy that extends from the house over the driveway, and serves as protection from the weather for an automobile and for people going between the house and the automobile. Used in a house with no garage. Also, a covering over a porch or patio, connecting two sections of a house or a house and a garage. It is open on two sides, allowing air circulation.

bridge loan
A short-term loan made to raise money for a special purpose. It is usually an interest-only, term loan, requiring a balloon payment. For example, the owners of a property who wish to purchase another property may create a bridge loan. The loan would be paid off with the profits from the subsequent sale of the first property.

bridging
The addition of small pieces of wood or metal, which are nailed in a diagonal position between floor joists, at mid-span, to prevent the joists from twisting.

British Thermal Unit (BTU)
A measurement of heat. One BTU is equal to the amount of heat required to raise the temperature of 1 pound of water 1 degree Fahrenheit at approximately 39.2° F. BTUs are used to measure the capacity of heating and air-conditioning equipment.

broker
One who acts for another in a transaction, for a fee or commission. A broker employs real estate agents and is responsible for their conduct.

broker buying as principal
A clause that is required in escrow documents when the buyer is a licensed real estate broker (salesperson) acting as a principal, for his or her own account. The seller must confirm knowledge of the fact.

brokerage
The occupation of a broker; the business of selling real estate through a broker who negotiates the sale for a commission.

broker representing both parties
A disclosure included in the escrow agreement, stating that both buyer and seller are aware of, and consent to, the broker representing both parties in the transaction.

brownstone
A type of row house constructed with reddish-brown sandstone, usually with little street frontage. Commonly built in the 19th century and located in large cities such as New York.

BTCF (before-tax cash flow)
The portion of net operating income after debt service is paid, but before income tax is deducted. Also called equity dividend or pre-tax cash flow.

BTU (British Thermal Unit)
A measurement of heat. One BTU is equal to the amount of heat required to raise the temperature of 1 pound of water 1 degree Fahrenheit at approximately $39.2°$ F. BTUs are used to measure the capacity of heating and air-conditioning equipment.

budget
A balance sheet that identifies estimated receipts and expenditures. A budget is crucial to business planning.

budget loan
A type of standard loan in which the monthly payments are applied to property taxes and insurance, as well as principal and interest. As a result, the borrower begins to build equity with the first monthly payment.

buffer zone
A term used in zoning to refer to the section of land that separates one land use area from another, especially when the two zones may be incompatible, such as industrial and residential areas.

building and loan associations
An obsolete term for savings and loan associations.

building capitalization rate
The capitalization rate historically used to estimate building value when using the land residual technique. The rate is the ratio of annual building income divided by the building value.

building codes
The minimum standards set for buildings and construction, for the protection of public safety and health. They are developed by the local, municipal or state government.

building lease
A long-term lease of raw land. The tenant agrees to pay a set ground rent, and also agrees to build and maintain a specified improvement.

building engineer
A person who inspects the structured components and the permanent systems of a building to ensure safety and compliance with all government regulations.

building line
A line beyond which there can be no construction. Set by law, the line prevents buildings from being built too close to the street, for safety and aesthetic reasons.

building permit
Written permission to construct a new building or other improvement, or to demolish or repair an existing structure. Building permits generally must be obtained before any work may be started.

building residual technique
An appraisal method used to determine the total property value. The income from the land is subtracted from the net operating income. The remainder is divided by the building capitalization rate and the result is the building value. The building value is then added to the land value to arrive at the total property value.

building restrictions
Limits put on the size or type of improvements allowed by zoning laws or private restrictions.

building standards
The types of construction elements the owner/developer uses when constructing or repairing a building.

build to suit
A type of lease arrangement in which the lessor builds or modifies the property to meet the tenant's specifications. The cost of the construction is figured into the rental amount, which is usually for a long term.

built-ins
Fixtures such as stoves, ovens, dishwashers, and other appliances, that are built into the walls and not movable.

built-up rate

A method of calculating the capitalization rate. It takes into consideration the yield amount each investor requires. Also called weighted rate. For example:

Investor 1 contributes 75% of the loan value and requires 9% interest.
Investor 2 contributes 15% of the loan value and requires 12% interest.
Investor 3 contributes 10% of the loan value and requires 10% interest.

$$0.75 \times 0.09 = 0.0675$$
$$0.15 \times 0.12 = 0.0180$$
$$0.10 \times 0.20 = \underline{0.0200}$$
$$\textbf{Total} = \textbf{0.1055}$$

or 10.55% weighted capitalization rate

bulk transfer law

Any transfer in bulk of a major part of the materials, inventory or supplies of an enterprise. The law states that the seller must report a bulk sale to the state tax authorities, and the purchaser must withhold payment until the seller's tax clearance is received.

bullet loan

A short-term, interest-only loan without periodic payments, with the entire loan due upon maturity. Generally, prepayment is not allowed, or not without large penalties.

bundle of rights

The various interests or rights an owner has in a property. These rights include the right to own, possess, use, enjoy, borrow against, and dispose of real property.

bungalow

A small one or one-and-one-half-story house.

business cycle
The constant fluctuation of levels of income, employment, and the amount of goods and services produced in one year. Stages of the cycle include prosperity, recession, depression, and recovery.

business opportunity
Any type of business that is for lease or sale.

business park development
A cluster of commercial properties. The properties may include warehouse space, research and development facilities or production space.

business risk
The uncertainty of future income of a business. In real estate, business risk includes variability in rents, vacancies, and operating expenses.

business valuation
The estimated worth of complete or partial ownership rights in a business.

butterfly roof
A roof formed by two gable roofs concave to a center ridge. The roof resembles the shape of a butterfly's wings.

buttress
A support for a wall. If the buttress projects from the wall and supports it by lateral pressure, it is called a "flying buttress."

buydown
A loan with an initially discounted interest rate that gradually increases to an agreed-upon fixed rate usually within one to three years. An initial lump sum is paid to the lender. This allows a buyer to qualify for more property with the same income.

buyer's broker
A broker who represents only the buyer's interests in a transaction.

buyer's market
A stage in the real estate market in which the ready, willing, and able buyer is in the minority and is in control of the market. A time of oversupply and decreased demand. Prices decline during this stage of the cycle.

buying power index (BPI)
A measure of demand in a certain area, relative to a given benchmark value. Common benchmarks are the United States and specific states or regions.

by-laws
Rules and regulations that govern the activities of a homeowner's association.

C

California Land Title Association (CLTA)
A trade organization of title companies in California.

California ranch architecture
A sprawling, one story, ranch-style building. Its interior layout is flexible.

call
In a metes and bounds description, the angle and distance of a given line or arc. Each call is usually preceded by the word "then" or "thence". For example, N 22° E 100' (1st call), thence N 80° E 100' (2nd call).

call option

A provision contained in loan documents that gives the lender the right to "call in," or make due immediately, the balance of the loan. The call can be exercised due to a breach of specific terms or conditions, or at the discretion of the lender.

Cal-Vet

The California Department of Veterans Affairs home loan program, funded by bonds under the California Farm and Home Purchase Act. Cal-Vet helps eligible California veterans to finance the purchase of farms and ranches within the state.

CAM (Certified Apartment Manager)

A designation offered by the National Apartment Association (NAA). The designation requires at least one year of apartment management experience, successful completion of a training program, and a community analysis project.

campanile

A freestanding bell tower.

CAMT (Certified Apartment Maintenance Technician)

A designation offered by the National Apartment Association (NAA). The designation requires at least one year of apartment maintenance experience, successful completion of a training program and passing score on final examination.

cancellation clause

Instructions in an escrow document about what to do if both buyer and seller agree to cancel the transaction, how monies are returned, who pays fees or charges incurred, and holding the broker harmless.

cantilever

A long bar or beam fixed at one end to a vertical support. It is used to hold a structure such as an arch, bridge or shelf in position.

capacity
Legitimate legal status to enter into a contract (mentally competent and of legal age), one of the legal essentials of a valid contract.

Cape Cod house
An adaptation of the New England style cottage. It may be one or two stories with a sloping roof, usually with dormer windows, cornices, and painted white frame.

capillary attraction
The force that allows porous material to soak up liquid.

capital
The money and/or property owned or used by a person or business to acquire goods or services.

capital assets
Property used to produce income, such as land, buildings, machinery, and equipment. In accounting, cash or property that can be easily converted to cash.

capital expenditure
The expense of investing in a capital asset such as purchases of land, buildings, or machinery. As opposed to expenses that are part of daily operations.

capital gain
The increase in value which may occur between the purchase and the sale of an asset. The taxable profit that is gained from the sale of that asset.

capital improvements
Any permanent improvement made to real estate for the purpose of increasing the useful life of the property or increasing the property's value.

capital loss
The decrease in value which may occur between the purchase and the sale of an asset.

capitalization
The process of calculating property value. The anticipated annual net operating income of the property is divided by the capitalization rate.

capitalization loss
A financial loss as a result of the sale of a capital asset.

capitalization rate
The rate of return an investor receives from an income-producing property. The rate is calculated using the property's net operating income divided by its value. It is also called the cap rate.

capricious value
An appraisal term that refers to value based on whim or emotion. It does not reflect fair market value.

caps
Limits placed on the amount the interest rate may vary during rate adjustments on variable-rate loans. The limits may be yearly or for the life of the loan.

CAPS (Certified Apartment Property Supervisor)
A designation offered by the National Apartment Association (NAA). Candidates must currently possess the Certified Apartment Manager (CAM) designation, or have at least four years of apartment management experience, including two years of multiple property management, successful completion of a training program, and passing score on final examinations.

capture rate
The estimated percentage of a total real estate market that is currently saturated by existing construction or is projected to be saturated by planned construction.

caravan
The inspection of newly listed properties by a group of real estate salespersons. Caravans usually occur on a regular basis and allow the salespeople a convenient opportunity to personally view each new property.

carport
An area, covered by a roof but open on the sides, which shelters a car. A carport may either extend from a structure (usually a house) or be constructed separately (often to accommodate several cars).

carryback financing
A sale of property in which the seller lends the money for part of the purchase price.

carrying charges
The various costs involved in property ownership including taxes, insurance costs, and maintenance expenses.

casement window
A window hinged at its sides, allowing it to swing open horizontally.

cash equivalency
The price for which real estate would sell if paid for in cash, without financing.

cash flow
The net income of an investment, after operating and other expenses are deducted from the gross income. A negative cash flow exists when the expenses are greater than income.

cash flow statement
A report showing cash flow after expenses are paid.

catwalk
A narrow, elevated walkway along a wall, or over a stage or other area where a person may need to go to operate or repair equipment.

caveat emptor
Latin for "let the buyer beware." A buyer purchases property at his or her own risk and is responsible for ensuring quality. In California real estate transactions, this principle has been replaced with the Disclosure Statement.

cavity wall
A wall constructed of brick or stone which is actually two separate walls, joined only at the top and the ends, making it hollow. Also called a hallow wall.

CBD (central business district)
The downtown area of a city containing primary business, retail, recreational, and governmental activities of the community.

CC&Rs (covenants, conditions, and restrictions)
Restrictions are placed on certain types of real property and limit the activities of owners. Covenants and conditions are promises to do, or not to do certain things. The consequence for breaking those promises may either be money damages in the case of covenants, or the return of the property to the grantor, in the case of conditions.

central business district (CBD)
The downtown area of a city, containing primary business, retail, recreational, and governmental activities of the community.

central heating system
A heating system consisting of four different elements: heat producer, exchanger, distributor, and controls. The system is designed to supply heat adequately for an entire structure.

CERCLA (Comprehensive Environmental Response, Compensation and Liability Act)
A law passed by Congress in 1980 that established two trust funds to help finance the cleanup of properties impacted by the release of hazardous wastes; commonly known as superfund.

certificate of eligibility
A document certifying that a veteran is eligible for a loan guaranteed by the Department of Veteran's Affairs.

certificate of occupancy
A certificate issued by a local building department to a builder stating that the building is in proper condition to be occupied.

certificate of reasonable value (CRV)
A document indicating the appraised value of a property being financed with a VA loan. The loan amount may not exceed the CRV.

Certified Apartment Maintenance Technician (CAMT)
A designation offered by the National Apartment Association (NAA). The designation requires at least one year of apartment maintenance experience, successful completion of a training program and passing score on final examination.

Certified Apartment Manager (CAM)
A designation offered by the National Apartment Association (NAA). The designation requires at least one year of apartment management experience, successful completion of a training program, and a community analysis project.

Certified Apartment Property Supervisor (CAPS)
A designation offered by the National Apartment Association (NAA). Candidates must currently possess the Certified Apartment Manager (CAM) designation, or have at least four years of apartment management experience, including two years of multiple property management, and completion of a training program.

certified check
A check bearing the issuing bank's guarantee that there is enough money on deposit to cover the check.

Certified International Property Specialist (CIPS)
A property management designation offered by FIABCI-USA (French acronym for International Federation of Property Managers and Real Estate Consultants). Candidates must successfully complete the CIPS Education program and exhibit expertise in international real estate.

Certified Leasing Specialist (CLS)
A designation offered by the International Council of Shopping Centers (ICSC). Candidates must have at least four years experience in shopping center leasing, or in lieu of the fourth year, the candidate may successfully complete an approved training program or prove they are a licensed real estate salesperson. In addition, the candidate must receive a passing score on a written examination.

Certified Manager of Community Associations (CMCA)
A designation offered by the Community Associations Institute (CAI). Candidates must successfully complete a 16-hour course and pass the National Certification Examination. Managers must adhere to the CMCA® Standards of Professional Conduct and obtain continuing education credits to remain certified.

Certified Marketing Director (CMD)
A designation offered by the International Council of Shopping Centers (ICSC). Candidates must have at least four years of shopping center marketing experience and pass an exam.

Certified Property Manager (CPM)
The most advanced property management designation offered by the Institute of Real Estate Management (IREM). Candidates must have a high school diploma, at least twelve months experience in property management, possess a current real estate license, complete a training program, pass an exam, and prepare a management plan.

Certified Shopping Center Manager (CSM)
A designation offered by the International Council of Shopping Centers (ICSC). Candidates must have at least four years of shopping center management experience and receive a passing score on a qualifying examination.

chain
A unit of measurement used by surveyors. One chain is equal to four rods, or 66 feet. Ten square chains of land equal one acre.

chain of title
A history of all documents affecting and transferring title of a property, beginning with the original transfer from government to private ownership, and ending with the latest document transferring title. Additional documents recorded in the chain include conveyances, liens, and encumbrances.

chalet
A style of housing design that originated in the Swiss Alps and is found mainly in mountainous vacation areas. The design features an A-frame with large, overhanging eaves that protect against heavy snowfall.

change, principle of
An appraisal principle stating physical or economic condition change over time, and those changes result in changing property values.

chattel
Any item of personal property.

chattel mortgage
A mortgage secured by personal property. These mortgages have now been replaced by security agreements.

chattel real
A personal property interest in real property, such as a lease. The lease itself is personal property, but it allows the holder to occupy real property.

check
A printed form, used instead of money, to make payments from a bank account.

chimney
Vertical masonry shaft of reinforced concrete or other noncombustible heat-resistant material that carries smoke and ash through the roof, away from the furnace or fireplace.

churning
The excessive sale and purchase of properties in order to gain financially.

CID (Common Interest Developments)
Real property developments that include common interests and shared common areas. One example of a CID is condominiums.

cinder block
A building block made of ashes and cement. Cinder blocks do not have the weight or the strength of cement blocks.

CIPS (Certified International Property Specialist)
A property management designation offered by FIABCI-USA (French acronym for International Federation of Property Managers and Real Estate Consultants). Candidates must successfully complete the CIPS Education program and exhibit expertise in international real estate.

circlehead window
A decorative semicircular window, usually above a door, which has no moving parts and is used to admit light.

circuit breaker
An electric fuse that activates and deactivates an electrical circuit when the current exceeds a safe limit.

civil law
Any laws that are not criminal laws; laws of civil or private rights. Violations of civil law include breach of contract, libel, and accidents.

clapboard
Narrow boards used as siding for frame houses, and having one edge thicker than the other. The boards run horizontally with the thicker edge overlapping the thinner edge.

classified ad
A small advertisement designed to give basic information. Usually found in newspapers and magazines.

classified property tax
Property tax that varies in rate depending on the use (zoning classification) of the property.

clean water act
A law passed by Congress in 1972 that prohibits the discharge of pollutants into natural waters.

clear headway
The height of the lowest overhead framing component (usually the top of a door frame) as measured from the floor.

clear span
An interior area of a building or house that does not use columns or posts to support the roof. This creates a large, open area with maximum visibility and use of floor space.

clear title
A title to a property that is free from any liens, clouds or defects.

clearing title
The process of identifying and removing any and all clouds or defects from a property's title.

clerk
A person in a hotel who is responsible for one or more specific functions, such as reservations or floor activities.

CLIC (Commercial Leasehold Insurance Corporation)
A corporation, owned by MGIC (Mortgage Guaranty Insurance Corporation), which provides leasehold insurance for commercial and industrial properties that do not have prime-rate tenants. The insurance guarantees that if the tenants do not pay their rent, the insurance company will.

client
The person who employs an agent to perform a service in exchange for payment.

client trust account
An account established to keep a client's monies separate from the broker's general funds. Also called an earnest money account.

closed bid
A real estate transaction that is not open for the usual negotiations. The bids from potential buyers are sealed until a specified time when they are opened and the seller picks the best offer. The seller benefits from this method because bidders often overbid to ensure their bid is chosen. Closed bidding is not a common practice.

closed cut valley
A roof valley where the shingles from one slope overlap the valley, and the shingles from the opposite slope are trimmed back from the valley centerline.

closed listing
A contract between a principal and an agent, giving the agent the exclusive right to market the principal's property for a fixed period of time. Also called an exclusive listing.

closed period
Regarding a mortgage, the period of time during which the loan cannot be prepaid.

closed mortgage
A mortgage that cannot be prepaid until a certain time or until maturity.

closed-end mortgage
A mortgage that cannot be used as security for additional loans.

closing
The act of finalizing the transaction in which the deed is delivered to the buyer, the title is transferred, and all costs are paid. Also called settlement.

closing costs
Expenses of the sale that must be paid in addition to the purchase price (buyer's expenses) or be deducted from the proceeds of the sale (seller's expenses).

closing statement
A summary of debits and credits prepared by a closing agent for the lender, borrower, seller, and buyer showing the details of the transaction.

cloud on title
Any condition that affects the clear title of real property. Examples include liens and encumbrances.

cloverleafing
A method of real estate canvassing by looping around the neighborhood or geographic area of a specific property (one recently listed or sold) in the shape of a cloverleaf, in order to obtain additional listings or buyers.

CLS (Certified Leasing Specialist)
A designation offered by the International Council of Shopping Centers (ICSC). Candidates must have at least four years experience in shopping center leasing, or in lieu of the fourth year, the candidate may successfully complete an approved training program or prove they are a licensed real estate salesperson. In addition, the candidate must pass an exam.

CLTA (California Land Title Association)
A trade organization of the state's title companies.

cluster development
An area of housing development in which the parcels are smaller than typical sites, and larger common areas are incorporated into the development.

CMCA (Certified Manager of Community Associations)
A designation offered by the Community Associations Institute (CAI). Candidates must complete a 16-hour course and pass the National Certification Examination. Managers must adhere to the CMCA® Standards of Professional Conduct and obtain continuing education credits to remain certified.

CMD (Certified Marketing Director)
A designation offered by the International Council of Shopping Centers (ICSC). Candidates must have at least four years of shopping center marketing experience and pass an exam.

coating
The application of a layer of material onto a surface, often a layer of viscous asphalt or other surfacing material.

code of ethics
A set of standards governing the conduct and judgment of professionals in their work.

codicil
A change in a will before the maker's death.

coinsurance
An insurance policy in which the insured must maintain coverage on a risk equal to at least 80 percent of its total value, or in the event of loss, suffer a penalty in proportion to the amount of the insurance deficiency.

collateral
Something of value given as security for a debt.

collateralized mortgage
A mortgage that is secured by something of value in addition to real estate. An existing mortgage used as security for another loan.

collusion
An agreement between two or more people to do something unlawful. Generally, an agreement between people who represent different interests and "sell out" these interests for personal gain.

Colonial architecture
Architecture that follows the style of New England colonial houses. The two story houses have windows divided into small panes, usually with shutters. The main façade is detailed and symmetrical, generally with a center entrance.

colonnade
A structure composed of a roof or series of arches supported by columns.

color of title
The false appearance of clear title, free of any clouds. The title actually has a certain defect, such as a forged deed, and as a result is invalid.

column
A slender upright structure consisting of a base, a round or square shaft, and a capital; a supporting or an ornamental member in a building.

combination door
An outer door using interchangeable panels of glass and screen, depending on the weather.

combination trust
A type of real estate trust that combines real estate investment trusts and real estate mortgage trusts. This allows the beneficiaries to earn rental income from the property, as well as mortgage interest and placement fees. Combination trusts are called balanced trusts in California.

combination window
A window using interchangeable panels of glass and screen, depending on the weather.

combustion
The reaction of a material with oxygen gas or other oxidant that produces heat, and often flame.

commercial bank
A financial institution designed to act as a safe depository and lender for many commercial activities.

commercial leasehold insurance
Leasehold insurance for commercial and industrial properties. Provided by the Commercial Leasehold Insurance Corporation (CLIC), the insurance guarantees that if the tenants do not pay their rent, the insurance company will.

Commercial Leasehold Insurance Corporation (CLIC)
A corporation, owned by MGIC (Mortgage Guaranty Insurance Corporation), which provides leasehold insurance for commercial and industrial properties that do not have prime-rate tenants. The insurance guarantees that if the tenants do not pay their rent, the insurance company will.

commercial paper
Short-term loans issued by banks and savings institutions for business enterprises. They are usually issued to companies with high credit ratings, thus the investment is almost always relatively low risk.

commercial property
A property where commerce is conducted, such as an office building or retail shopping center.

commingling
The depositing of client funds in the broker's personal account; a prohibited practice.

commission
An amount paid to the broker at the close of escrow. The amount is agreed upon before the transaction takes place and is usually a percentage of the purchase price.

commissioner
A member of a state real estate commission; a person chosen to decide how to partition a property among co-tenants; or, a person appointed to supervise a mortgage foreclosure sale.

commission split
The division of commission funds between the broker and sales associate. The split ratio is agreed upon before the sales transaction takes place.

commitment
An agreement or pledge to do something; especially to assume a financial obligation.

commitment fee
A charge imposed by a lender for holding credit available for a borrower to use at a future date.

common area
An area of land, or an improvement, that is owned by the owners or tenants of a complex or subdivision, especially a condominium, for the common use of residents.

common interest
The portion of the common areas that each condominium apartment owner owns. The portion of ownership is usually determined by a ratio of the size of the individual apartment unit to the total square footage of all the apartment units. The size of the portion determines the amount the owner will be assessed for maintenance, operation, and taxes of the common properties.

Common Interest Developments (CID)
Real property developments that include common interests and shared common areas. A condominium is an example of a CID.

common law
A law based on what is generally accepted, used, and customary, rather than on legislation.

common wall
A wall that is shared by two or more buildings or by 2 or more units in the same building.

community apartment project
One type of CID in which the owner has an undivided interest in the land with the exclusive right to occupy a particular unit.

community center
A retail center anchored by a small department store and supported by up to 50 smaller stores. At least 5,000 households are needed to support a community center.

community property
Property that is held jointly by a husband and wife. In California, all property acquired by a married couple is presumed to be community property, unless otherwise stated in a written agreement. Community property includes all earned income and assets purchased with community property monies.

Community Reinvestment Act (CRA)
Legislation enacted by Congress in 1977 to require banks and other lenders to make capital available in low- and moderate-income urban neighborhoods, in order to stabilize these declining areas. Lenders, developers, and property owners have been reluctant to finance redevelopment of these areas, for fear of being held environmentally and financially liable for cleaning up these sites.

comparables
Properties that are similar to a subject property and are used in the appraisal process. Also referred to as comps.

comparison
An appraisal method of determining the capitalization rate of a property by looking at the operational capitalization rate of similar properties in the area.

comparison approach
An appraisal method of determining property value by looking at the sale prices of comparable properties. Also called the direct market comparison, direct sales comparison, or market data approach.

comparative-unit method
An appraisal method used to determine the value of a building by multiplying the cost per square foot of a recently built comparable building by the number of square feet in the subject building.

compensable damages
Money that must be paid to the owner of a property totally or partially condemned under the government's powers of eminent domain. The amount of damages is based on the value of the property lost, rather than on sentimental value, inconvenience, or loss of business not directly related to the real estate.

competent party
A person entering into a contract who is legally capable to enter into such a binding contract. Criteria for competency include age of majority and mental capacity.

competition, principle of
An appraisal concept that states that profitability attracts competition, which may in turn decrease profitability.

competitive area
The geographic area in which competition for a subject property occurs and may affect its revenues, expenses, and value.

competitive differential
The process of identifying the features of one property that give it a competitive edge over other properties. The information is derived from a survey of the competition.

competitive market segment
A group of similar properties that are in the same market area and compete directly with the subject property.

completion bond
A guarantee by an insurance company that a builder will complete a construction project.

compliance clause
A clause in a lease agreement designating the laws with which each party must comply.

compound interest
Interest calculated on the principal plus accrued interest.

Comprehensive Environmental Response, Compensation and Liability Act (CERCLA)
A law passed by Congress in 1980 that established two trust funds to help finance the cleanup of properties that have been impacted by the release of hazardous wastes and substances; commonly known as superfund.

compressor
An electro-mechanical device used to circulate refrigerant through a refrigeration system.

concentric zone theory/model
A theory of land development stating that cities grow by adding rings around existing rings of activity. At the center of the rings is the Central Business District. The next ring contains manufacturing, warehousing, and low-end commercial activities. The next ring contains low-income housing. As the rings continue outward, the level of housing increases.

concessions
Discounts or enticements given by a landlord or seller to attract prospective tenants or buyers into signing a lease or purchasing property.

concierge
An employee in a large hotel who makes special arrangements for guests, such as obtaining theater tickets.

concrete
A mixture of cement, sand, aggregate, and water used as a structural material.

concurrent ownership
Ownership of a piece of property by two or more persons at the same time. Examples of concurrent ownership include joint tenants, tenants by entirety, tenants in common, and community property owners.

concurrent recording
When the closing of an escrow is contingent upon the simultaneous closing of another escrow.

condemnation
The process by which the government acquires private property for public use, under its rights of eminent domain. The property owner is owed fair compensation for the condemned property.

condensation
The cooling of a gas or vapors into a liquid state. It appears as a film or water droplets.

condenser
The refrigeration mechanism that converts gaseous refrigerant back into a liquid state.

condition of sale
A comparison factor used in the direct sales comparison approach of appraisal. It refers to the motivations of the buyer and seller in the sales transaction. Examples are the relationship between buyer and seller, financial needs, and lack of market exposure.

condition precedent
A condition that requires something to occur before a transaction becomes absolute and enforceable. For example, a sale may have a condition precedent requiring the buyer to obtain financing.

condition subsequent
A condition which, if it occurs at some point in the future, can cause a property to revert to the grantor. For example, a condition subsequent in a grant deed may require the buyer to use the property only as a private residence. If they later use it for a business, it reverts to the original owner.

conditional sales contract
A contract in which the seller retains the title, but possession is given to the buyer. If the buyer defaults on the contract or any of its conditions, the property is returned to the seller. Also called an executory contract.

condition
A limiting restriction in the ownership of real property, the violation of which could cause the owner to lose title or have the estate modified in some way.

condominium
A type of CID. A structure for residential, industrial or commercial use where there is an undivided interest in common in shared areas, as well as a separate interest in the individual unit.

condominium ownership
Ownership of property that is made up of an individual interest in an apartment or commercial unit, and an undivided common interest in the common areas.

conduction (thermal)
The transmission of heat through the passage of energy from particle to particle.

conductor (thermal)
A substance that facilitates the transfer of heat by means of conduction.

conduit
Plastic or metal tubing that houses electrical wiring. Also, a means of transmitting or distributing something.

conformity, principle of
An appraisal concept that states that the greatest value is realized when buildings in a certain neighborhood are similar in design, construction, and age.

congruous
Suitable or appropriate. In appraisal, describes a property that is suitable to the area.

connector
Device used to join an electrical wire to a piece of equipment or another wire.

consequential damages
Payment made to compensate for a breach of contract. Also, damage to a parcel of land done by a public body or adjacent owner that impairs its value.

consideration
Anything of value; one of the essentials of a valid contract.

consistent use
An appraisal concept that states that land and improvements must be valued on the same basis. Improvements must contribute to the land value in order to have any value themselves.

consolidate
To combine or bring together.

constant

A percentage of the original loan that is paid in equal annual payments over the life of the loan. For example, a $1 million loan with a 10.8 percent constant requires a $108,000 annual payment.

constant amortization mortgage

A mortgage that requires equal periodic payments on the principal. As the loan is amortized over time, the interest decreases, and the total payments decrease.

constant payment mortgage

A mortgage with fixed payments of principal and interest for the life of the loan.

construction cost

The cost of building a structure including labor, materials, contractor's overhead and profit, taxes, and construction loan interest. Construction cost is different from original cost, which is the price the owner paid, which may be more or less than the construction cost.

construction loan

A short-term, interim loan to finance the cost of construction. The loan money is disbursed in increments as construction progresses.

constructive notice

Knowledge of a fact that is a matter of public record. The law presumes that everyone has knowledge of that fact. The opposite of actual notice.

constructive trust

A trust created when a person obtains title to property and/or takes possession of it and holds it for another, even though there is no formal trust document or agreement. The court may determine that the holder of the title holds it as a constructive trustee for the benefit of the intended owner. This may occur through fraud, breach of faith, ignorance or inadvertence. Also called involuntary trust.

contemporary architecture
A general term used to describe modern building designs that do not conform to any traditional architectural styles.

contiguous
Touching, connecting, or adjoining. In the case of subdivisions, non-adjoining plots of land may still be considered contiguous by their inclusion in a common promotion or sale.

contingency
A provision in a contract that requires the completion of a certain act or the occurrence of a particular event before that contract is binding. An example of a contingency is the buyer obtaining financing.

contingency listing
A type of property listing used in a multiple-listing service that has unusual or special conditions that must be met.

contingent liability
Responsibility that extends beyond personal actions or deeds.

continuing education
Most states require real estate and appraisal licensees to take additional classes and training prior to license renewal or reinstatement.

contract
A legal document that states and explains a formal agreement between two people or groups, in exchange for consideration; also the agreement itself.

contract documents
In real estate, the papers that explain and serve as proof of the agreement entered into by the buyer and seller.

contract for deed

A contract to purchase real property in which the seller agrees to defer all or part of the purchase price for a specified period of time.

contract of sale

A contract for the sale of real property in which the seller gives up possession but retains title until the entire purchase price is paid in full.

contract rate

The agreed-upon interest rate of a loan, adjusted for inflation. Also called the nominal rate.

contract rent

The amount of rental income due from the tenant as agreed in the lease agreement.

contractor

A person or company supplying materials or work, for a set price, in the construction industry. Since the individual or company is not a regular employee, they receive no benefits.

contractual intent

Intent to enter into a contract. Also an action that may be understood by another party to imply intent to enter into a contract. A clear understanding of intent will prevent jokes and jests from becoming valid contracts.

contribution, principle of

An appraisal concept that any property improvement, regardless of its actual cost, is worth only what it adds to the property's market value.

convection

The transfer of heat in water, air, or another fluid, as the substance descends when it is cooler, and rises when it is warmer.

convention hotel
A large hotel designed to accommodate conferences with thousands of guests.

conventional loan
A long-term loan that is not insured or guaranteed by a governmental agency. The loan typically requires a substantial down payment and is usually available only to those with good credit. It has fixed monthly payments for the life of the loan and usually has a 30-year period of fixed interest rates.

conversion
The acquisition or taking of property belonging to another.

convertible loan
An adjustable-rate loan that allows the borrower to change to a fixed rate at any time during the life of the loan.

convey
To transfer ownership or title.

conveyance
The transfer of title to property from one person to another by use of a written instrument.

cooling-off period
A period of time after entering into a contract in which either party may legally back out of the contract.

cooperating broker
A real estate broker who assists another broker by finding a buyer for a property.

cooperative

A residential multifamily building. A trust or corporation holds the title, and the residents are the beneficiaries. Each resident possesses a proprietary lease. All owners have joint liability for the mortgage on the property.

copies

Copies of all documents that must be given to buyer and seller at the time of signing.

corner influence

The affect on property value that a corner lot location produces. The value may be greater or less than inside lots, depending on the perceived benefits of being located on a corner.

corner lot

A potential building site located at the intersection of two streets.

cornice

The top molding or façade of an exterior or interior wall. Used for decorative purposes.

corporation

An entity or organization whose rights in business are similar to that of an individual. It exists indefinitely, has centralized management in a board of directors, shareholder liability is limited to the amount of their individual investment, and corporate stocks are freely transferred.

corrections and deletions

A requirement that any corrections and deletions made in a document must be approved by all principals.

correlative water right

A law exercised in some states restricting riparian owners who share a common water source to taking a reasonable amount of the total water supply.

correspondent
Another name for a mortgage banker.

corrosion
The gradual wearing away of a metal by rusting or chemical usage.

co-signer
A joint signer of a contract or note. The individual becomes obligated to the agreement along with the principal party.

cost
The amount paid for goods or services.

cost approach
An appraisal method used to determine property value. The value is calculated by subtracting depreciation from the cost of replacing or reproducing a property's improvements, and adding the estimated land value.

cost basis
The original price paid for a property.

cost of living index
A government indicator of the fluctuating cost of living for an average person on a monthly basis.

cost recovery
The deduction of value from an income-producing property over a period of time. Similar to depreciation. However, cost recovery is not limited by the "useful life" of the property. The entire cost of the property may be deducted over a certain period of time.

cost to cure
The dollar amount necessary to restore a deteriorated item to new or reasonably new condition.

cost-benefit ratio

The ratio of the benefits of an improvement to the cost of that improvement. In order for the improvement to be considered desirable, the ratio must exceed 1.00.

cottage

Originally, a house with no surrounding land belonging to it. In modern times, cottage refers to a small house, perhaps used as a seasonal home.

counteroffer

In a real estate transaction, the rejection of an original purchase offer and the submission of a new and different offer.

coupon bonds

A type of bond that features coupons, or interest payments, which are cashed periodically by the holder of the bond. Also known as bearer bonds.

court

A short road or open area, partially or wholly enclosed by buildings. Also, a judicial body that hears legal cases.

court confirmation

The approval by a court of the sale of property by an executor, administrator, guardian, conservator or commissioner in a foreclosure sale. The property may continue to be marketed by a broker, and others may represent different competitive bidders until confirmation is received. If court confirmation is not obtained by the date shown in the instructions, the buyer may cancel this agreement by giving written notice of cancellation to the seller.

covenant

A promise or agreement to do, or not do, something that is set forth in a written agreement. A form of private restriction. It is one of the CC&Rs.

covenant of seisen

A clause in a mortgage document which guarantees that at the time of conveyance, the grantor owns and possesses the property and has the authority to sell it or hold it as collateral.

covenant running with the land

A covenant that becomes part of the property rights and transfers to successive owners. The covenant must be in writing, "touch and concern" the land, it must have been the intention of the creators that it run with the land, and subsequent owners must be notified of the covenant.

covenants, conditions, and restrictions (CC&Rs)

Restrictions are placed on real property and limit the activities of owners, and/or uses of the property. Covenants and conditions are promises to do, or not to do, certain things. The consequence for breaking those promises may either be money damages in the case of covenants, or the return of the property to the grantor, in the case of conditions.

CPM (Certified Property Manager)

The most advanced property management designation offered by the Institute of Real Estate Management (IREM). Candidates must have a high school diploma, at least twelve months experience in property management, possess a current real estate license, successfully complete a training program, pass a qualifying examination, and prepare a management plan.

CRA (community reinvestment act)

Legislation enacted by Congress in 1977 that requires banks and other lenders to make capital available in low- and moderate-income urban neighborhoods, in order to stabilize these declining areas. Lenders, developers, and property owners have been reluctant to finance redevelopment of these areas, for fear of being held environmentally and financially liable for cleaning up these sites.

crack

A break or split without complete separation, generally caused by stress or ground movement.

Craftsman architecture

A style of architecture popular in California between 1900 and 1920. Craftsman homes are generally 1½ stories with a long, sloping roofline and a wide, pillared porch. The pillars typically widen at the base. Other typical features include a tile or stone fireplace, dark, heavy woodwork, and beamed ceilings.

crawlspace

Approximately four feet of space between the ground and the floor of some homes, to provide access to wiring, plumbing, etc.

creative financing

Financing techniques that are atypical. Creative financing may have different principal amounts, interest rates, or payment terms.

credit loan

A mortgage that is granted based upon the financial strength of a borrower, not taking into consideration equity or collateral.

credit rating

An estimate of the credit worthiness and responsibility of a consumer. The rating is given by various credit agencies. Also, the amount, type, and terms of credit that are considered safe to extend to a consumer.

credit report

A document listing the credit history of an individual. Lenders use it as an indicator of the strength of an individual's credit.

credit union
A cooperative, non-profit organization established for banking purposes. Credit unions offer their members (usually a group of teachers, workers, government employees, etc.) higher interest rates than at other savings institutions. Credit unions are usually used for savings accounts and short-term loans, but occasionally make longer-term loans secured by real property, such as second mortgages.

cricket
A peaked structure, which diverts water at the point where a roof meets a chimney or another slope.

cross-collateralization
When collateral for one loan also serves as collateral for one more additional loans.

cross connection
The line connecting two piping systems, one of which contains potable water and the other containing non-potable water or another fluid. There may be a flow from one system to the other, and the direction of flow depends on the pressure differential between the two systems.

cross-defaulting clause
A clause usually included in a secondary loan contract that stipulates that a default in the primary loan will also cause a default in the junior loan.

crown molding
A type of large molding with a curved face and beveled edges, used on a cornice or to cover the angle where the wall meets the ceiling around a room.

crunch down

The recasting, or rewriting, of a loan at a lower balance, in order to help a distressed borrower avoid an impending foreclosure. The lender absorbs the loss, as it is estimated to be less than the cost of foreclosure.

CRV (certificate of reasonable value)

A document indicating the appraised value of a property being financed with a VA loan. The loan amount may not exceed the CRV.

CSM (Certified Shopping Center Manager)

A designation offered by the International Council of Shopping Centers (ICSC). Candidates must have at least four years of shopping center management experience and pass a qualifying examination.

cubic foot cost

The cost of reproduction calculated by multiplying the number of cubic feet of a property by the construction cost per cubic foot.

cul-de-sac

A street or alley that is open at one end only, with a large, rounded, closed end to facilitate U-turns. Usually found in subdivisions.

cumulative discount rate

The cumulative effect of landlord lease concessions on gross rental rates. It is expressed as percentage of base rent.

curable depreciation

Depreciation that is physically and financially feasible to correct.

curb appeal

The good or bad impression of a property one gains from an initial viewing, usually while driving by or standing on the curb.

curtail schedule
A schedule for payment of a mortgage, showing the amount of each payment, the payment number, interest payment, principal payment, and unpaid principal balance. Sometimes referred to as an amortization schedule.

curtilage
The grounds and additional buildings surrounding a house that are commonly used in connection with the everyday use of the house. Usually fenced.

custodian
One who is entrusted with the care and keeping of real or personal property on behalf of another.

customer
A prospective buyer, or client.

cycle
The ups and downs that occur in a period of time.

D

damages
Compensation that a plaintiff may be paid as a result of injuries to himself or his property, through an act or default of another. Complex laws determine the amount of damages awarded.

damage or destruction clause
A clause in a lease detailing how the partial or total destruction of the property would be handled between the parties to the lease.

date
The exact date a legal document or contract is signed. Certain documents may have several dates that indicate when different aspects of the agreement will take place or take effect.

date of acceptance
The date the seller accepts the offer or the buyer accepts the counteroffer.

date of appraisal
The date on which the opinion of value applies. The date of appraisal is not necessarily the same as the date the report is written. Also called the valuation date or date of value.

date of closing
The date the title of a recently sold property is transferred to the buyer.

date of value
The date on which the opinion of value applies. The date of appraisal is not necessarily the same as the date the report is written. Also called the valuation date or date of appraisal.

debenture
A bond backed only by the credit of the borrower, and not secured by a mortgage or lien on property. The debt is recorded by an indenture agreement.

debit
The opposite of a credit. An entry on an accounting statement or balance sheet showing an amount owed.

debt equity ratio
The ratio of the total loan amount to the total amount of equity possessed by the owner.

debt ratio
The difference between an individual's debt payments and their monthly income.

debt service
The periodic payment specified in the loan contract necessary to repay the total amount of debt.

debtor's position
The value of a property over the amount of the borrower's mortgages. Also called equity.

decedent
A dead person. Usually one who has died recently.

deck
The surface installed over the supporting framing members to which the roofing material is applied. Also, an outdoor, uncovered porch-type structure, usually connected to a house.

declaration
A legal document that must be filed by condominium developers in most states. The declaration describes the land to be developed, and the resulting condominiums, the type of lease, and other legal requirements.

declaration of homestead
A recorded declaration that protects, up to a certain amount, a home and the adjoining land against certain money judgments.

declaration of restrictions
A list of all the covenants, conditions, and restrictions that are tied to a parcel of land.

declining annuity
Evenly spaced, periodic payments that are decreasing in amount. Also called decreasing annuity.

decreasing annuity

Evenly spaced, periodic payments that are decreasing in amount. Also called declining annuity.

dedication

The voluntary transfer of private property for public use.

deed

A legal document that is the official record of an agreement or official proof of ownership of real property.

deed in lieu of foreclosure

A deed conveying mortgaged property that is in default. The owner deeds the defaulting mortgage to a lender to avoid foreclosure action. It is also called a voluntary deed or voluntary conveyance.

deed in trust

A form of deed in which a trustor places property in the hands of a trustee to manage on behalf of the trustor, or for a beneficiary. Deeds in trust are usually used to create land trusts.

deed of trust

Like a mortgage, real property is given as security for a debt. However, in a deed of trust there are three parties to the instrument: the borrower, the trustee, and the lender (beneficiary). The borrower transfers the legal title for the property to the trustee who holds the property in trust as security for the payment of the debt to the lender or beneficiary. Also called a trust deed.

default

Failure to pay a contractual debt.

default clause

A clause in a lease specifying the lessor's rights, and the possible penalties facing the lessee, in the event of a default.

default interest rate
A higher interest rate that is charged on a loan, if certain terms or conditions are not fulfilled by the borrower, such as a loan default.

default judgment
A judgment entered in favor of the plaintiff when the defendant defaults, or fails to appear in court.

defeasance clause
A clause included in a loan agreement that cancels the mortgage upon repayment of the debt in full. The title to the property is transferred back to the mortgagor, and the lender's interest in the property is terminated.

deferred maintenance
Negligent care of a building. Putting off necessary maintenance for a time, resulting in physical depreciation and loss of value.

deficiency
A feature of a property considered faulty or insufficient.

deficiency judgment
A judgment against a borrower for the balance of a debt owed when the security for the loan is not sufficient enough to pay the debt.

deflation
A state of the economy when price levels decrease and purchasing power increases.

de la Cuesta
The precedent-setting case (Fidelity Federal Savings v. de la Cuesta) in which the U.S. Supreme Court ruled that the due-on-sale clause was legally enforceable. The due-on-sale clause is contained in mortgage documents and states that the loan becomes due if the property is sold.

delinquency
The failure of a borrower to make payments on time, as specified under a loan agreement.

delivery
Transfer of property from one to another.

demand letter
A letter, generally sent from a lawyer, warning a borrower who is behind in payments on a loan, that unless the loan is made current within a certain period of time, the lender will consider the borrower to be in default on the loan. The letter details how and when the loan must be paid, and potential legal action.

demise
In real estate, to convey real property to someone for a certain length of time, as in a lease; to let.

demographic
Information regarding the size, density, and distribution of human populations that is useful to appraisers in performing analyses of potential land use and value.

demolition cost
The expense required to demolish a building. It may be used in an appraiser's highest and best use analysis.

density zoning
A type of zoning ordinance that restricts the average number of houses per acre that may be built within a specific subdivision. This average is called gross density.

Department of Real Estate (DRE)
The department of the state government responsible for the licensing and regulation of real estate salespeople. The person heading the department is usually called the Real Estate Commissioner. Other names for the department are the Division of Real Estate and the Real Estate Commission.

Department of Veterans Affairs (DVA)
Established in 1944, the DVA guarantees a portion of an eligible veteran's loan.

depletion
A reduction in the value of an asset due to the removal or exhaustion of a resource or material.

deposit increase in cash
A clause in escrow documents declaring that the amount of the initial deposit will be increased in a certain number of days after acceptance of the agreement.

deposit
Money that is given to show intent to follow through with a purchase agreement. It is given along with an offer to purchase. Also called earnest money.

deposit receipt
Also known as a sales contract; the primary document used to present an offer on real property.

Depositor Institutions Deregulation and Monetary Control Act of 1980
The federal legislation that ended regulation of the banking industry. Prior to the legislation, the Federal Reserve required member banks to hold a certain amount of their assets in a form that did not earn interest. As this was costly to bank profits, many new banks were opened as state banks, which are exempt from the Federal Reserve's law. The decline in member banks worried government policy makers, and was the impetus for the deregulation.

depreciable rate
The rate at which an asset loses a limited resource or material.

depreciable real property
Property that is used as a business or produces income, and is subject to wear and tear.

depreciation
The loss of value of a property due to age, physical deterioration, functional or economic obsolescence, or other factors.

depreciation reserve
An account into which the estimated replacement cost of equipment is accumulated each year over the life of the asset, so it can be replaced when it becomes obsolete and totally depreciated. Commonly used in the accounting of public utilities.

depression
A rare stage in the business cycle following a recession characterized by extremely high unemployment and very little purchasing power.

deregulation
A process by which financial institutions that formerly had been restrained in their lending activities by the law are allowed to compete freely for profits in the marketplace.

description
A section of a conveyance document that legally defines the property to be transferred. The property is generally described in two ways; first, by general location such as a street address. Then the property is described specifically, using public or plat maps, or other recorded information.

development
The process of planning and building on an area of land. During development, property values may be established and/or may increase.

development rights
The right to build on or improve a property. The rights may be sold separately from the land.

devise
A gift of real property by will. Also, the giving of a gift of real property using a will.

devisee
A person who receives land or real property in the last will and testament of the donor.

dew point
The temperature at which dew starts to form, or vapor to condense and deposit as a liquid.

direct capitalization
One of two types of capitalization. It is determined by capitalizing the net operating income of a property from a certain period of time.

direct endorsement program
An FHA special program allowing eligible lenders to consider mortgage applications without first submitting paperwork to HUD for approval. This makes it easier and quicker for low- and moderate-income families to buy homes.

direct sales comparison approach
A method of property appraisal that most directly uses the principle of substitution. The appraiser finds three to five comparable properties that have recently sold, notes any dissimilar features and makes a price adjustment for each. The appraiser then assigns a value to the subject property based on the adjusted sales price of the comparable property that is most similar.

disclaimer
A statement denying legal responsibility for the product sold. It is also a denial or renunciation of one's legal right to property.

disclosure

The act of showing, or making something known. In real estate, it is an important risk reduction tool used by brokers.

disclosure statement

A required statement that lists all the information relevant to a piece of property, such as the presence of radon or lead paint. Also, it is a written statement of a borrower's rights under the Truth-in-Lending Law, or a statement of all financing charges in a transaction, which must be disclosed by a lender.

discount

The difference between the full amount and the lesser amount paid. When the holder of a long-term loan or material goods sells for less than face value in order to get cash quickly, the difference in value is the discount.

discount rate

The interest rate charged by the Federal Reserve Bank to its member banks for loans. Changes in this rate have a significant impact on the real estate market. Also the percentage of discount charged by a bank for purchasing loans or commercial paper in advance of the date of maturity.

discretionary income

The portion of an individual's income available for investment or spending after the necessities (rent or mortgage, food, clothing, etc.) have been paid.

discrimination

In real estate, the illegal practice of violating someone's right to fair housing opportunity on the basis of race, color, sex, religion, familial status, marital status, disability or national origin.

disintermediation

The process of depositors removing funds from savings.

display ad
A large, expansive ad that may use graphics and pictures to tell a more complete story. Often used to advertise property in large apartment complexes with frequent vacancies.

disposable personal income
An individual's total income for spending or investment, after deductions for taxes.

distressed property
Property that is in poor financial or physical condition; foreclosed real estate or property in a bankruptcy; income property that is performing poorly.

divest
To sell; to release one's interest in a property.

dividend
A number to be divided by another.

doctrine of correlative user
A law exercised in some states, restricting riparian owners who share a common water source to taking a reasonable amount of the total water supply.

dominant tenement
The property that benefits from an easement. For example, the property which benefits from a beach access trail through another's property is considered the dominant tenement. Also called dominant estate.

door attendant
An employee in a large hotel who assists guests through entrances and exits and keeps foot traffic moving.

door jamb
The framework surrounding a door or door opening.

dormer
A projection from the roof of a building, usually a house, which contains a window. The projection is built at an upright angle from the slope of the roof.

double escrow
Two escrows on the same property, at the same time, having the same party as buyer and seller of the property. For example, Escrow 1: Alex buys from Bob. Escrow 2: Alex immediately sells the same property to Carl. Alex is using Carl's money to buy Bob's property. The process is illegal in many states unless full disclosure is made.

double-hung window
A window that opens vertically from the top and bottom, containing two separate sashes with a locking device, usually at the center where the top of the lower sash meets the bottom of the upper sash.

double net lease
A lease arrangement in which the tenant pays the rent, utilities, property taxes, special assessments, and insurance premiums.

double pitch
The most common roof design used for houses. The roof comes to a crest at the center and slopes away in two directions.

down payment
The portion of a property's purchase price paid in cash at the time the sale agreement is executed; the portion of the purchase price that is not financed.

downspout
The pipe or duct used to carry rainwater from a gutter to the ground. Also called a leader, this vertical portion of the gutter system carries water away from the house, preventing basement leaks.

downtown hotel
An older hotel located in the center of a large city. It may be limited in space, thus may offer luxury amenities to entice travelers.

downzoning
A change in a zoning standard reducing the usage allowed for the property. An example of downzoning is reducing a property's usage from residential to conservation.

draft curtains
Fire retardant partitions usually made of sheet metal or dry wall that are attached to the interior of a roof, dividing a building in order to prevent the spread of fire within the building.

drain
A channel or pipe for drawing off water or sewage in a building drainage system.

drainage
The system of gutter and drainpipes used to carry water away from the foundation of a home.

draws
Monetary advances made to a borrower.

DRE (Department of Real Estate)
The department of the state government responsible for the licensing and regulation of real estate salespeople. The person heading the department is usually called the Real Estate Commissioner. Other names for the department are the Division of Real Estate and the Real Estate Commission.

dry mortgage
A lien that places no personal liability on the mortgagor or his or her personal assets, using only the property as security.

dry rot
Wood decay due to fungi, caused when wood is subjected to a constant source of moisture. Dry rot appears as brown, crumbling wood.

drywall
An interior wallboard made of any number of materials other than plaster, such as gypsum board, plywood or wood paneling.

dual agency
An agency relationship in which a real estate salesperson represents both buyer and seller in a transaction. Some states require written consent before a broker may act as dual agent.

dual contract
A contract between two parties who have made two contracts for a single transaction. One of the contracts is fraudulent and is often used to obtain a larger loan than previously available.

duct
Thin sheet metal, shaped either round, square or rectangular, which is used to convey air at low pressure.

due on encumbrance
A rarely used clause in mortgages that allows the lender to foreclose if the borrower gets additional financing, such as a second mortgage.

due-on-sale clause
A provision in a mortgage that states that the balance of the loan is due if the property is subsequently sold.

duplex
A residential building containing exactly two units. The units are either side by side, sharing a common wall and roof, or stacked one above the other.

duress
The use of force to achieve agreement to a contract.

Dutch door
A door divided horizontally into halves. The halves may open and close independent of the other, or they may be latched together to act as one door.

DVA (Department of Veteran's Affairs)
Established in 1944, the DVA guarantees a portion of an eligible veteran's loan.

dwelling
Any shelter used for long-term residence; house, abode.

E

early occupancy
A situation in which the buyer is allowed to take possession of a property before the closing of escrow. This arrangement has a high risk for problems and is not recommended.

earnest money
A cash deposit paid by the prospective buyer of real property to demonstrate his or her good-faith intention to complete the sales transaction. The amount of earnest money is generally less than 10 percent of the purchase price. It is not essential to make a purchase agreement binding.

easement
The right to use another's land for a specified purpose; sometimes known as a right-of-way.

easement appurtenant
An easement that runs with the land.

easement in gross
An easement that is not specific to any one parcel; for example, public utilities.

eave
The lower section of the roof forming an overhang and comprising a fascia, soffit, and soffit molding.

ECOA (Equal Credit Opportunity Act)
Legislation passed in the mid-1970's, that made lender discrimination based on age, gender, national origin, marital status, religion and race illegal.

economic base analysis
The study of economic forces that affect a certain community. The analysis is used to predict population, income, and other variables that may affect real estate or land use.

economic forces
In appraisal theory, one of several types of forces that affect property values.

economic life
The period of time a property is reasonably functional and useful.

economic obsolescence
A loss in value due to changes outside the property, which negatively affect the property. Examples of economic obsolescence are the relocation of a major industry, or changes in zoning. Also called external obsolescence.

economic rent
The amount for which a leased property would be expected to rent, under current market conditions if the property were vacant and available for rent.

economic rent increase
An increase in rent prompted by a shrinking supply of comparable rental units in an area and the ability of tenants to afford the increase.

economically feasible
One of the four criteria for determining highest and best use. In order for a use to be considered highest and best, it must be able to produce sufficient income to repay the expenses involved in creating it, and provide the owner with a return on investment.

economics
Related to real estate, a study of the factors that cause people to prosper and create a viable demand for real property.

effective age
The age of a building based on its physical condition, and not its chronological age.

effective gross income (EGI)
The total income a property can produce, less any anticipated expenses or deductions. Also known as adjusted gross income.

effective rate
The interest rate a borrower actually pays on a loan, as opposed to the nominal rate that is stated in the loan contract. If the interest rate is computed on the total loan amount over the total life of the loan, and then added to the principal before the monthly payments are calculated, the interest rate may end up being greater than what was stated in the loan agreement.

efflorescence
A white, powdery substance that appears on masonry or concrete due to the surfacing of salts in the material.

effluent
Septic system liquid waste.

EGI (effective gross income)
The total income a property can produce, less any anticipated expenses or deductions. Also known as adjusted gross income.

egress
The way one exits a property; the opposite of ingress.

EIR (Environmental Impact Report)
A study of how a development will affect the ecology of its surroundings.

electrostatic precipitator
A device that removes pollution and particles in the air. It gives the particles an electrical charge, collects them on filters that have the opposite charge, thereby removing them.

elevator operator
An employee in a large period hotel who operates the elevator, adds authenticity and keeps traffic moving. Nearly obsolete.

eluviation
The movement of soil, caused by excessive water in the soil.

emancipated minor
Someone who is underage, yet legally set free from parental control/supervision. Emancipation may be achieved by marriage or by court order.

emblements
Annual crops produced for sale. Considered personal property.

eminent domain
The right of a local, state or federal government to acquire private property for public use. The government must pay the owner fair market compensation for the acquired property.

encroachment

The unlawful intrusion of one property owner's permanent improvement on the adjacent property owned by another. Chain-of-title generally does not reveal encroachments, thus they are not warranted against in a standard title insurance policy; such protection would require an extended-coverage title policy. One example of an encroachment is a wall erected between neighboring properties.

encumbrance

A claim or liability that attaches to a property, and limits the value or negatively affects that property's title or use. There are two distinct classifications of encumbrances. Encumbrances may affect the title, such as judgments, mortgages, mechanic's liens, and other liens, which are charges against the property used to secure a debt or obligation. Encumbrances may also affect the physical condition of the property, such as restrictions, encroachments, and easements.

endowment

A form of permanent financial support. Donors establish endowment funds to provide permanent income.

English architecture

A general term used to describe various English housing styles. The exterior is usually characterized by large stones, or exposed timbers with large stones or brick placed between the timbers. The roof is most often of slate and windows are hinged vertically.

entitlement

Eligibility; the degree to which a veteran deserves to receive a DVA loan.

entrepreneur

A person who attempts to make a profit by starting their own company or by operating alone in the business world, and thereby assumes a substantial portion of the risks, profits, and losses.

Environmental Impact Report (EIR)
A study of how a development will affect the ecology of its surroundings.

Environmental Protection Agency (EPA)
A federal agency established in 1970 to ensure the enforcement of the National Environmental Policy Act (NEPA).

Equal Credit Opportunity Act (ECOA)
Legislation passed in the mid-1970's that made lender discrimination based on age, gender, national origin, marital status, religion and race illegal.

equilibrium
A status achieved when opposing characteristics of land in a specific market balance each other out. Also, when supply and demand in a market balance each other and prices stabilize.

equitable rights
The rights of an individual to occupy, lease or sell a property.

equitable title
The right to obtain absolute ownership to property when legal title is held in another's name. A buyer may sue in equity for performance if a seller refuses to transfer the property once a contract of sale is signed. The buyer has a right to demand that title be conveyed upon payment of the purchase price. The right is transferable by deed, assignment, subcontract or mortgage, and passes to the vendee's heirs upon death.

equity
The value remaining in a property after payment of all liens. Also called debtor's position.

equity dividend
The portion of net operating income after debt service is paid, but before income tax is deducted. Also called before-tax cash flow or pre-tax cash flow.

equity loan
A loan made using the equity in the borrower's home as security. The equity is based on a percentage of the appraised value of the home.

equity of redemption
The right of a debtor, before a foreclosure sale, to reclaim property that had been given up due to mortgage default. Also known as the right of redemption.

equity ratio
The percentage of a property that is unencumbered by debt. Calculated by dividing the equity interest of a property by its total value.

equity trust
An investment trust that deals in owning real estate rather than in financing. One example of an equity trust is the Real Estate Investment Trust (REIT).

erosion
The gradual wearing away of land by natural processes.

errors and omissions (E&O) insurance
A form of professional liability insurance. It protects business owners and professionals against liability claims or lawsuits for damage caused by errors, mistakes, and negligence.

escalation/escalator clause
A clause in a lease that allows for rent increases based on the occurrence of a certain event, such as an increase in inflation.

escheat
The reversion of a property to the state or county, if the owner dies intestate (without a will) or without heirs.

escrow
The closing of a real estate transaction. Funds and documents are deposited with a neutral third party who is instructed to carry out the provisions of the agreement.

escrow instructions
A document, signed by a buyer and seller in a sales transaction, which explains the closing procedures and requirements of the escrow agent.

escrow holder
An independent third party legally bound to carry out the written provisions of an escrow agreement; a neutral, bonded third party who is a dual agent for the principals; sometimes called an escrow agent.

estate
A right or interest in property, and the degree, quantity, nature, and extent to which a person has that right or interest.

estate at sufferance
A situation where a tenant has come into possession of property in a lawful manner but has stayed beyond the prescribed duration of the agreement, hostile to the owner's wishes. For example, a tenant who initially signed a lease, but has stayed on the property after the lease has expired, against the wishes of the landlord or owner.

estate at will
A tenancy agreement that endures as long as both parties are willing. It can be terminated at any time, by either party.

estate for years
A tenancy agreement for a definite period of time. It could be for any period of days, weeks, months or years. If the tenancy lasts for more than one year, the agreement must be in writing.

estate from period to period
A leasehold estate that is automatically renewed for the same term; a conveyance for an indefinite period of time; it does not need to be renegotiated upon each renewal; an example is a month-to-month rental.

estate in fee
The most complete form of ownership of real property. It is of indefinite duration and may be inherited and transferred. Also known as an estate of inheritance.

estate of inheritance
A freehold estate that can be passed by descent or by will after the owner's death. A type of estate in fee.

estate tax
A federal or state tax charged on the transfer of an individual's assets inherited by heirs. Also called an inheritance tax.

estoppel
A legal doctrine which prevents a person from denying something to be true or a fact if the denial is contrary to previous statements or actions made by that same person. For example, in boundary disputes, a landowner is often estopped from claiming that the true boundary line is different from a line previously agreed on by the owner and his or her neighbor. This is especially true if the neighbor, relying on the landowner's representations of the line's location, built a fence or driveway.

ethics
A set of principles or values with which an individual guides his or her own behavior and judges that of others.

evaporator coil
A device used in refrigeration. It is made of a coil of tubing, and is used to evaporate refrigerant.

eviction
The legal process by which the tenant is removed from the property due to violations of terms of the lease.

exception
The exclusion of some part of the property to be sold. Also, the liens and encumbrances that are not included in the coverage of a title insurance policy.

exchange: agree to cooperate
A statement in tax deferment escrow documents, declaring that buyer and seller agree to cooperate with each other to complete the transaction, and that neither party is to pay any additional expenses or be liable in connection with the other party's tax deferred exchange.

exclusionary zoning
A type of illegal zoning which intentionally or unintentionally excludes racial minorities and low-income residents from an area.

exclusive agency
An employment agreement between an agent and a principal. The principal gives the agent the exclusive right to market and sell the principal's property for a fixed period of time. The principal may still sell his or her own property under this agreement, without any commission being due to the agent.

exclusive listing
A contract listing a property for sale that gives one agent the exclusive right to market that property for a fixed period of time. Also called a closed listing.

exclusive right to sell
A written listing agreement appointing a broker the exclusive agent for the sale of property for a specified period of time.

exculpatory clause
A clause in a mortgage that limits the options for recourse of one party against another in the event of a default.

execute
To perform or complete; to sign.

executed contract
A contract in which the obligations have been performed on both sides of the contract and nothing is left to be completed.

executive manager
An executive who oversees the entire operation of a property management firm.

executor/executrix
A person named in a will to handle the affairs of a deceased person.

executory contract
A contract in which obligation to perform exists on one or both sides of the contract.

expansible house
A house specifically designed for later additions or expansion.

expedientes
Land grants recorded by the Mexican government in California in the early 19th century.

expense
The cost of goods and services.

express contract
A contract created when the parties declare the terms and put their intentions in words, either oral or written.

express warranty
An obligation to a tenant created by a promise made by the landlord or landlord's agent that caused the tenant to enter into the lease.

expropriation
The seizure of private land for a public purpose under the government's right of eminent domain. The property is condemned and fair market compensation is paid to the owner.

extended policy
An extended title insurance policy.

extension
An agreement to continue an action or contract beyond an initial period. A lease extension prolongs the lease agreement for an additional period of time beyond its original term.

external obsolescence
A loss in value due to changes outside the property, which negatively affect the property. Examples of external obsolescence include zoning changes, proximity to nuisances, and changes in land use or population. Also called economic obsolescence.

extraction
An appraisal method of calculating land value. The value is achieved by deducting all improvement costs (less depreciation) from the sales price. Also called allocation or abstraction.

extrapolation
The process of predicting future trends based on current and past patterns and relationships. It assumes that the same economic factors that influenced past trends will affect future trends similarly.

eye appeal
Aesthetic appeal. A property's amenities and features such as landscaping or a pleasant view.

F

façade
The outer or front face of a structure. Often used to describe an exterior that features a unique design.

face value
The stated amount of a bond or security, as opposed to its market or real value.

Facilities Management Administrator (FMA)
A property management designation offered by the Building Owners and Managers Institute (BOMI) with emphasis on the management of a commercial facility.

Fair Housing Amendment Act of 1988
An amendment to the Federal Fair Housing Act. The act made housing discrimination based on physical or mental handicaps illegal, as well as discrimination against those with children under the age of 18.

fair housing laws
The general designation given to laws originating in the United States Constitution ensuring all persons the fair opportunity for housing of their choice in the United States.

Fair Labor Standards Act
A federal law that guarantees a worker's right to be paid fairly. The law established the 40-hour workweek, sets the federal minimum wage and requirements for overtime, and places restrictions on child labor.

fair market value
The price a property would bring if freely offered on the open market with both a willing buyer and a willing seller.

Fannie Mae (Federal National Mortgage Association)
Federal National Mortgage Association, the nation's largest mortgage investor. The company buys mortgages from lenders and resells them as securities on the secondary mortgage market.

Farm Credit System
A separate national banking system that finances the needs of farmers, ranchers, rural homeowners, agricultural cooperatives, rural utility systems, and agribusinesses. Unlike other banks, Farm Credit System banks and associations do not take deposits. Instead, funds that can be loaned are raised through the sale of System-wide bonds and notes in the nation's capital markets.

Farmers Home Administration (FmHA)
A relief agency that disburses emergency farm financing. It complements the activities of the Farm Credit System by creating and insuring loans to farmers who are unable to obtain financial assistance from other sources.

fascia
Horizontal, flat trim pieces that are used around the outer end of roof rafters at eave and wall junctures.

FDIC (Federal Deposit Insurance Corporation)
A federal agency that insures depositors in banks and savings and loan associations to protect their deposits in case of bank failure.

feasibility study
An analysis performed on a proposed property to determine potential income and expenses, and most effective use and design. Often used by developers to entice investors. Some mortgage investors and lenders require a feasibility study before they will grant a loan.

Fed (Federal Reserve System)
The federal agency that helps maintain healthy credit conditions nationwide to counteract inflation and deflation; creates conditions favorable to high employment, stable values, internal growth, and rising levels of consumption; and regulates member banks.

Federal Deposit Insurance Corporation (FDIC)
A federal agency that insures depositors in banks and savings and loan associations to protect their deposits in case of bank failure.

federal fair housing law
Enacted in 1968, the law prohibits housing discrimination based on race, color, sex, familial status, handicap, religion or national origin.

federal funds rate
The interest rate the Fed charges to member banks on unsecured loans.

Federal Home Loan Bank System (FHLB)
Manages and regulates savings and loan associations, as the Federal Reserve System regulates the commercial banking industry.

Federal Home Loan Mortgage Corporation (Freddie Mac)
A stockholder-owned company which buys mortgages from lending institutions, pools them with other loans, and sells shares to investors.

Federal Housing Administration (FHA)
A federal agency established in 1934 that encourages improvements in housing standards and conditions, provides an adequate home-financing system, and exerts a stabilizing influence on the mortgage market.

Federal Open Market Committee (FOMC)
Directs and regulates the Federal Reserve System's open-market operations. Open-market operations consist of the bulk sale and purchase of government securities.

Federal Reserve System (Fed)
The federal agency that helps maintain healthy credit conditions nationwide to counteract inflation and deflation, creates conditions favorable to high employment, stable values, internal growth and rising levels of consumption, and regulates member banks.

Federal Savings and Loan Insurance Corporation (FSLIC)
Now defunct, it once provided account insurance and supervised operations of its member savings and loan associations.

federal tax lien
A lien placed on a taxpayer's real property, by the federal government, if the owner has not paid their taxes or is in violation of federal income tax or payroll tax laws.

fee
A type of estate; the maximum possible estate one can possess in real property. It is of indefinite duration, freely transferable and inheritable. Examples are fee simple, and estate in fee. A fee may also be a charge for labor or services provided. The buyer and seller in a real estate transaction generally share the fees involved in the transaction.

fee appraiser
A professional appraiser who is not employed by a particular fiduciary lender; an independent appraiser. Also known as a field appraiser.

fee simple absolute
The maximum possible estate one can possess in real property. It is of indefinite duration, freely transferable and inheritable. Also known as fee simple, or fee.

fee simple defeasible
An ownership estate limited by restrictions and conditions. If the agreement is breached, the title may be returned to the seller or his/her heirs. Also known as fee simple qualified.

fee simple estate
The greatest interest one can have in real property. It is unqualified, indefinite in duration, freely transferable and inheritable.

fee simple qualified
An estate of ownership limited by restrictions and conditions. If the agreement is breached, the title may be returned to the seller or his/her heirs. Also known as fee simple defeasible.

fee simple
The largest, most complete ownership recognized by law, also known as a fee simple absolute, or fee.

felt
Fibrous material, saturated with an asphalt compound, that is used under roof shingles or flashing for water resistance.

fenestration
The decorative manner or plan of placing doors or windows in a structure.

FHA (Federal Housing Administration)
A federal agency established in 1934 that encourages improvements in housing standards and conditions, provides an adequate home-financing system, and exerts a stabilizing influence on the mortgage market.

FHLB (Federal Home Loan Bank System)
Manages and regulates savings and loan associations, as the Federal Reserve System regulates the commercial banking industry.

FHLMC (Federal Home Loan Mortgage Corporation)
A stockholder-owned company that buys mortgages from lending institutions, pools them with other loans and sells shares to investors. Also known or Freddie Mac.

fictitious deed of trust
A recorded deed of trust that contains general terms and provisions but names no specific parties and describes no property; it is used for reference only.

fiduciary
A type of relationship that implies a position of trust or confidence. Also, a person who holds assets in trust for a beneficiary, or who stands in a position of trust, confidence, and/or responsibility for another.

fief
Rights in the land that become heritable.

file
The act of placing an original document on public record.

filter
A device used for separating solid particles, impurities, etc. from a liquid or gas by passing it through a porous substance.

final value estimate
An appraisal term that refers to the range of value or dollar amount given at the end of an appraisal report that has been calculated by reconciling the different appraisal methods of valuation used in the appraisal.

finance charge
Interest and any other charges, including points, that make up the fees incurred when borrowing money.

finance fee
A fee a mortgage brokerage charges to the borrower to cover expenses when creating a mortgage with their institution.

financial analysis
A study of a property's income producing performance and potential.

financial institution
A public or private organization that collects funds and invests them in financial assets, or lends them back out in order to earn a profit.

Financial Institutions Reform, Recovery and Enforcement Act (FIRREA)
Legislation enacted in 1989 as a result of the savings and loan crisis, to ensure another such disaster does not occur. FIRREA established the Office of Thrift Supervision.

financial intermediary
An organization that obtains funds through deposits and then lends those funds to earn a return. Examples include savings banks, commercial banks, credit unions, and mutual savings banks.

financial service center
A center that provides customers with a variety of financial services, such as insurance, real estate sales, real estate loans, and banking services, in one location.

financial statement
A document showing the financial status, net worth, credits, and debits of a person or company.

financing
The act of loaning and borrowing money in order to buy an item. Also, the various fees and charges incurred when borrowing money.

financing statement
A written notice filed with the county recorder by a creditor who has extended credit for the purchase of personal property; it establishes the creditor's interests in the personal property, which is the security for the debt.

finder's fee
A reward paid to someone who finds a willing and able buyer for a real estate transaction. Also called a referral fee.

fine-tune
A technique used by the Fed to manipulate the nation's economy by controlling the amount of money in circulation.

fire stop
A wooden block built between the wall studs or joists, within covered walls, which closes off the passage of air, thereby limiting the spread of fire.

FIRPTA (Foreign Investment in Real Property Tax Act)
A federal law requiring nonresident aliens and foreign corporations to pay U.S. income tax on gains earned from the sale of U.S. real property interest.

FIRREA (Financial Institutions Reform, Recovery and Enforcement Act)
Legislation enacted in 1989 as a result of the savings and loan crisis, to ensure another such disaster does not occur. FIRREA established the Office of Thrift Supervision.

first mortgage
A loan that takes priority over all other loans. Also called a senior loan.

fiscal year
The financial year that starts on July 1 and runs through June 30 of the following year; used for real property tax purposes.

fixed assets
Assets that are not easily converted into cash.

fixed capital
Money that is invested in fixed assets or property.

fixed costs
Expenses that occur regularly, regardless of changes in business activity. Examples are property taxes, rent, insurance, and maintenance.

fixed-rate loan
A loan whose interest rate never changes for the life of the loan.

fixed window
A window that has no moveable parts, such as a picture window.

fixture
Any personal property attached to land on a semi-permanent or permanent basis that becomes real property once attached.

fixtures and equipment
Part of an escrow agreement stating that the seller guarantees that fixtures and equipment shall be in working condition at the time of buyer's possession.

flag lot
A potential building site whose configuration looks like a flag on a pole. It is generally located behind another lot, with an access road or driveway extending through and to one side of the front lot, and reaches the main road. The access road represents the flag pole.

flagstone
A decorative, flat, slate-like stone, used in walkways and patios, and processed in a variety of colors.

flashing
Waterproof sheets of plastic or corrosion-resistant metal, installed along with exterior finishing materials for the prevention of water leakage in such places as the intersection of a wall and roof or the valley of a roof.

flat lease
A lease in which equal payments are made at set intervals throughout the life of the lease.

flexible payment mortgage
A loan with graduated payments. Initially, the interest rates are lower than ordinary loans, thus the initial payments are lower, enabling younger or less wealthy buyers to purchase property. The payments then increase for a period of time, before leveling off at a stable rate.

flood insurance
Insurance that covers damage from floods or tidal waves. Primary and secondary lending institutions require flood insurance on any financed property within certain areas identified by the Federal Emergency Management Agency (FEMA) as being flood-prone. The insurance premium is a fixed amount.

flood hazard zone
An area prone to flooding. In order to obtain any loan secured by a property in such a zone, the buyer must purchase flood insurance.

floodplain
Land that is subject to periodic flooding due to its proximity to a river and because it is level.

floor duty
A common practice in real estate offices of assigning one sales agent the responsibility of handling all walk-ins and phone calls from prospective buyers and sellers who are not clients of a specific agent. Floor duty is rotated among the agents, often on a daily basis.

flue
The opening or passageway in a chimney through which smoke, gases, and ash pass from a building.

flue liner
Heat resistant lining, usually of fire clay or terra cotta pipe, used for the inner lining of chimneys.

FMA (Facilities Management Administrator)
A property management designation offered by the Building Owners and Managers Institute (BOMI) with emphasis on the management of a commercial facility.

FmHA (Farmers Home Administration)
A relief agency to disburse emergency farm financing. It complements the activities of the Farm Credit System by creating and insuring loans to farmers who are unable to obtain financial assistance from other sources.

FNMA (Federal National Mortgage Association)
The nation's largest mortgage investor. The company buys mortgages from lenders and resells them as securities on the secondary mortgage market. Also referred to as Fannie Mae.

FOMC (Federal Open Market Committee)
Directs and regulates the Federal Reserve System's open-market operations. Open-market operations consist of the bulk sale and purchase of government securities.

footing

The base or bottom of a foundation pier, wall, or column that is usually wider than the upper portion of the foundation. The footing transfers the structural load to the ground.

forbearance

A refrain from action by a creditor against the debt owed by a borrower after the debt has become due.

force majeure

A force that cannot be resisted or controlled. Includes acts of God, and acts of man (riots, strikes, arson, etc.). The term is used primarily in insurance, but may also be used in any type of performance contract, such as construction.

forced sale

The sale of property due to the debtor's inability or unwillingness to make payments on the loan.

foreclosure

The process of selling a debtor's property in the event of default on a mortgage or other lien, in order to repay the remaining debt.

foreclosure sale

A sale where property is sold to satisfy a debt.

Foreign Investment in Real Property Tax Act (FIRPTA)

A federal law requiring nonresident aliens and foreign corporations to pay U.S. income tax on gains earned from the sale of U.S. real property interest.

forfeiture

Relinquishing rights to something due to nonperformance of an obligation or condition. A delinquent borrower may lose the rights to property due to forfeiture.

forgery
The illegal falsification of a signature or document, making an entire contract void.

Formica®
A type of hard plastic formed into thin sheets, which are then used primarily for counter-tops in kitchens and bathrooms.

forms
Documents that provide written evidence of agreement, activity, policy, and responsibility.

for sale by owner (FSBO)
Attempting to sell a property without listing with a broker. Many owners in this situation will cooperate and compensate a broker who ultimately represents a buyer.

foundation
The support structure of a house. The base or portion of a structure that is in contact with the ground, usually extending below grade.

foyer
A large entrance or reception area located just inside the front entrance of a building, such as in a theater or hotel; also found in many homes.

fractional appraisal
An appraisal of only a portion of a property. The appraisal may be of a leasehold interest in the property, or of a particular improvement.

frame house
A wood-sided house.

framing
Construction of the framework of a house, made up of studs, rafters, joists, and beams.

franchise
The right to operate a business, using another company's name and products. A recent trend in the real estate industry is the franchised brokerage, such as Century 21 and ERA.

fraud
An act meant to deceive someone in order to get them to part with something of value.

Freddie Mac (Federal Home Loan Mortgage Corporation)
A stockholder-owned company that buys mortgages from lending institutions, pools them with other loans, and sells shares to investors.

free and clear title
A title that is unburdened by any liens, clouds or other encumbrances.

freedman
In medieval times, a status of citizenship that allowed a person to own land.

freehold estate
Ownership rights and interests in real property that continue for an indefinite period of time. May be passed on to the owner's heirs after death.

Freon®
The trade name of a type of gas used as a cooling agent in refrigerators and air conditioners.

fresco
A method of painting on wet plaster on a wall. As it dries, the paint becomes part of the wall and remains much longer than if simply painted on a dry plaster wall.

front-end ratio
The ratio of all housing expenses to gross income.

front-end zero
A type of Private Mortgage Insurance recently initiated in California. Instead of paying the insurance premium up front, the borrower can finance the entire premium, making installment payments over the life of the loan, as if it were interest.

front footage
The width of a property along a street.

front money
A down payment. Money that a borrower must pay up-front.

front-of-the-house
Operations of the hotel business that deal directly with guests. Front-of-house positions include bellhop, front desk, and doorman.

FSBO (for sale by owner)
Attempting to sell a property without listing with a broker. Many owners in this situation will cooperate and compensate a broker who ultimately represents a buyer.

FSLIC (Federal Savings and Loan Insurance Corporation)
Now defunct, it once provided account insurance and supervised operations of its member savings and loan associations.

fuel oil
A liquid or liquefiable petroleum product that is used to generate heat or power.

full disclosure
The requirement to reveal any and all relevant facts pertaining to a property. A broker is legally obligated to full disclosure.

full reconveyance
The transferring of property by a lender, to a borrower, once the mortgage debt has been completely repaid.

fully amortized note
A note that is fully repaid at maturity by periodic reduction of the principal.

functional obsolescence
A loss of value from defects in a building or structure due to layout, design or other undesirable features.

funding fee
A fee charged to the veteran borrower when securing a DVA guaranteed loan.

fungi
One of a large group of thallophytes living in damp wood, which include mold, mildew, rust, mushrooms, etc. They are parasites that live on organisms or feed on dead organic material. They lack true roots, stems, leaves, and chlorophyll, and reproduce by means of spores.

furring
Wood or other material that is applied to a surface prior to attaching wallboard or other wall covering panels.

fuse
A safety device in an electrical system such as a strip of easily melted metal. The strip is set in a plug, which is placed in a circuit as a safeguard so that, if the current is too strong, the metal melts and breaks the circuit, to avoid fire.

future worth
The increased value of money over time.

G

gable
In roof construction, the triangular area above the eaves between two sloping rooflines.

gable roof
A roof design using rafters cut to the same length and joined in the center to form a peak, with two sides of the roof sloping down from that peak. An example of a gable roof can be found on page 261.

gallery
In architecture, a covered walkway, open on one side, running along an upper story of a building, either inside or outside.

galvanized
A protective coating added to metal to inhibit corrosion or oxidation by hot dipping the metal in zinc or electroplating it.

gambrel roof
A roof style with two different slopes from the ridge to the eaves. The lower slope is steeper than the upper flatter slope. This roof is often used on barns. An example of a gambrel roof can be found on page 261.

gap analysis
An analysis of the difference between a market's supply and demand.

gap financing
A short-term, high-interest loan that helps to bridge a possible gap between available bank loans and the total amount of required financing. Gap financing is usually used for machinery, equipment, leasehold improvements, inventory, or working capital for start-up or business expansion.

gazebo
A small structure with a roof and open sides, usually in the garden, where one may sit and enjoy the view. Also called a belvedere.

GDP (Gross Domestic Product)
A measure of the US economy adopted in 1991; the total market values of capital and goods and services produced within the United States borders during a given period (usually 1 year).

GEM (growing equity mortgage)
A mortgage that has a fixed interest rate and increasing monthly payments. The increased payments are put towards the loan principal. GEMs allow you to pay mortgages off earlier, save in interest payments, and build equity quickly.

general contractor
A construction specialist who negotiates construction contracts with developers to construct a building or other real estate project. He or she must pass an examination to obtain a license from the state regulatory agency. The general contractor may work with subcontractors as well, who specialize in different aspects of the construction process. Also called the prime contractor.

general ledger
A report showing an accounting of all debits and credits passing through the business bank account for various periods of time.

general lien
A lien that affects all the property owned by a debtor, rather than a specific property. A general lien may be created either by the courts, by issuing a judgment, by creditors, or through federal and state tax liens.

general maintenance workers
Workers in various trades hired from time to time to keep a building running smoothly.

general manager (hotel)
The top manager in charge of all departments of a hotel.

general obligation bonds
A type of municipal bond which are funded from property taxes and used for public improvements such as public utilities, prisons or schools.

general partner
In a limited partnership situation, the individual or company who acquires, organizes, manages, and is primarily liable for the investment.

general partnership
A form of business in which partners share in liability and income. The income, gains, and losses are passed through to individual partners who pay tax on their own income. The organization has right of survivorship. This form of ownership is best for small groups of investors.

gentrification
The process of purchasing, renovating, and rehabilitating properties in an older, run-down neighborhood.

geodetic survey system
A method of legal land description used for very large areas. The entire country is marked by a network of benchmarks located by latitude and longitude. It is a variation of the rectangular survey system.

Georgian architecture
A style of architecture dating back to the 18th century. Characterized by first floor windows extending to the ground, with doors and windows of simple and well-balanced design, yet formal in appearance.

Georgian colonial architecture
A more formal and elaborate form of Georgian architecture.

gerrymander
To divide an area into districts, without using any obvious natural divisions, for an unlawful purpose. For example, dividing a school district to keep out certain people for reasons of race or religion.

GFCI (Ground Fault Circuit Interrupters)
A safety device to protect against electrical shock by cutting off the flow of electricity when there is even a slight stray of current leakage.

gift deed
Used to make a gift of property to someone, usually a close friend or relative.

gift tax
A federal tax imposed on a donor making a gift. A gift is considered to be the transfer of any type of property for less than what the property is really worth. The gift tax is applicable to gifts worth more than $10,000.

gingerbread work
Ornamentation in a building's (usually residential) architecture, which adds to aesthetic appeal, rather than functional value.

Ginnie Mae (Government National Mortgage Association)
A division of HUD. It funds high-risk mortgages for high-risk borrowers, typically in areas approved for government construction projects that have no other funding sources. Like Fannie Mae and Freddie Mac, Ginnie Mae also buys home loans issued by others and, after pooling them together, sells shares to investors. However, unlike Fannie Mae and Freddie Mac, Ginnie Maes are backed by the United States government and thus have a higher credit standing.

going concern value
The value of a business while in operation, apart from its real estate and assets.

good consideration
Gifts such as real property based solely on love and affection.

good faith
Bona fide; an act that is done honestly, whether it is actually negligent or not. Recording laws protect "good faith" purchasers. Acts committed in "bad faith" are often punishable as a crime.

goodwill
An intangible, saleable asset arising from the reputation of a business; the expectation of continued public patronage.

Government National Mortgage Association (Ginnie Mae)
A division of HUD. It funds high-risk mortgages for high-risk borrowers, typically in areas approved for government construction projects that have no other funding sources. Like Fannie Mae and Freddie Mac, Ginnie Mae also buys home loans issued by others and, after pooling them together, sells shares to investors. Unlike Fannie Mae and Freddie Mac, Ginnie Maes are backed by the United States government and thus have a higher credit standing.

government survey method
A method of legal land description using east-west lines (base lines) and north-south lines (principal meridians). Additional lines are drawn 6 miles apart and are known as township lines (east-west) and range lines (north-south). Also called the rectangular survey method.

governmental forces
One of four forces believed to affect real estate value in appraisal theory. Examples of governmental forces are government controls and regulations, zoning and building codes, and fiscal policies.

GPAM (Graduated Payment Adjustable Mortgage)
A loan in which the monthly payment graduates by a certain percentage each year for a specific number of years, then levels off for the remaining term of the loan.

grace period
An agreed-upon time period after the payment of a debt is past due, during which a party can repay the debt without being considered in default.

graduated lease
Sometimes called a step-up lease, usually a long-term lease with an escalation clause allowing for a rent increase based upon the occurrence of a certain event.

Graduated Payment Adjustable Mortgage (GPAM)
A loan in which the monthly payment graduates by a certain percentage each year for a specific number of years, then levels off for the remaining term of the loan.

grandfather clause
A clause in a law permitting the continuation of a use or business which, when established, was permissible but, because of a change in the law, is now not lawful. Commonly used in zoning ordinances.

grant deed

A deed containing an implied promise that the person transferring the property actually owns the title and that it is not encumbered in any way, except as described in the deed. This is the most commonly used type of deed.

grant deed from spouses to create separate estate

A disclosure statement in escrow documents executed by the wife or husband of the grantee, that relinquishes any community property interest he or she may have in the subject property.

grantee

The person receiving the property, or the one to whom it is being conveyed.

granting clause

The clause in a deed or mortgage that conveys the property.

grantor

The person conveying, or transferring, the property.

green properties

Hotels that participate in the AH&MA's environmental management program.

gross density

The average number of houses allowed per acre under density zoning ordinances.

Gross Domestic Product (GDP)

A measure of the US economy adopted in 1991; the total market values of capital and goods and services produced within the United States borders during a given period (usually 1 year).

gross income

The total annual income produced by a property, before expenses are deducted.

gross lease
A lease arrangement in which the lessee pays a fixed rent while the lessor pays all the property charges such as repairs, taxes, insurance and operating expenses.

gross living area
The total living space of a home, generally represented by the habitable, finished, above-grade floor space. Calculated by measuring the building's outside perimeter.

gross rate
The interest rate charged on a mortgage, which includes servicing fees, before any tax deductions are taken.

gross rent
Income (figured annually) received from rental units before any expenses are deducted.

gross rent multiplier
A number which, when multiplied by the gross income of a property, yields an estimate of property value.

Ground Fault Circuit Interrupters (GFCI)
A safety device to protect against electrical shock by cutting off the flow of electricity when there is even a slight stray of current leakage.

ground rents
Payment for the right to occupy and use a piece of land. The owner still owns the ground, and the tenants must pay rent to use and possess the building existing on the land. Often referred to as economic rent.

grout
Thin mortar used in masonry work to fill joints between bricks, blocks, or tiles.

growing equity mortgage (GEM)
A mortgage that has a fixed interest rate and increasing monthly payments. The increased payments are put towards the loan principal. GEMs allow you to pay mortgages off earlier, save in interest payments, and build equity quickly.

guarantee of title
An assurance of clear title.

guest ranch
A lodging accommodation providing a unique vacation experience for a guest who participates in ranch life.

gutter
Horizontal channels which are installed at the edge of a roof to carry rainwater away from the house.

H

hard money loan
The evidence of a debt that is given in exchange for cash. A type of non-conventional loan. Hard money loans are quick and the terms are flexible. The loan is based upon the sale of the assets, without significant regard to the borrower, or the borrower's financial strength. The lender will also generally overlook clouds such as foreclosures, bankruptcies, judgments, and outstanding mortgages. Borrowers with a profile that traditional, conforming lenders will not service. Hard money loans are usually funded at a higher cost to the borrower in exchange for the ease and speed of obtaining this type of funding.

hardwood
Wood that is used for interior finish, such as oak, maple, and walnut.

hazard insurance
Insurance that covers physical damage done to property by fire, wind, storms, and other similar risks. Sometimes earthquakes and floods are also covered.

hazardous waste
Toxic waste material that jeopardizes the value of real estate.

header
The top horizontal piece, often made of boards nailed together, which serves as the top section of a window or door and carries the wall load.

hearth
The area in front of, and around, a fireplace. Usually constructed of brick, stone or tile.

heat exchanger
An apparatus that transfers heat from one fluid to another in cooling or heating systems. Air conditioners use both a condenser and an evaporator. Steam and hot water radiators are heat exchangers, which are used to produce heat.

heating, ventilation, and air-conditioning (HVAC)
A system that regulates the distribution of fresh air and heat throughout a building.

hectare
A metric measurement of land equal to 100 ares (10,000 square meters) or 2.471 acres.

hereditaments
Things that are capable of being inherited.

highest and best use
The use of land that produces the most profit or amenities. There are four criteria in determining highest and best use: physically possible, legally permissible, economically feasible, and maximally productive.

hip roof
A roof with four sloping sides that rise to a ridge. Usually found on garages or church steeples. Also called a pyramid roof. An example of a hip roof can be found on page 261.

historic district
A zoning classification that refers to a geographic area recognized to have historical significance.

holdback
A portion of the loaned funds not advanced by a lender until the borrower meets specific requirements and/or conditions. In construction lending, a percentage of the contractor's loan funds are withheld until the construction is completed.

holder
The party to whom a promissory note is made payable.

holder in due course
A person who has obtained a promissory note or other negotiable instrument, without knowledge that it is defective, or was dishonored at the time it was negotiated. The holder must have obtained the note in good faith, as a result of an ordinary business transaction, before the note is due, and given something of value for it. The holder is entitled to payment by the maker of the check or note. The holder is protected from any claims, made by the maker, that the check or note has already been paid. For his own protection, the maker should have the note marked "paid" and returned to him to prevent the holder from transferring the note to another holder, who then could force the maker to pay it again.

holding escrow
A sales agreement in which the escrow agent holds the final title documents to a contract for deed. At the time of the sale, the seller gives the escrow agent an executed deed, and instructs the agent to deliver the conveyance to the buyer when the contract obligations are fulfilled. This is an advantageous arrangement if the seller is uncooperative or unable to be located when the buyer is ready to make full payment on the debt. It can be problematic, however, if the escrow agent cannot determine if and when the contract obligations have been completely fulfilled, if the seller has died or remarried, or if the buyer has resold the property.

holdover tenant
A tenant that retains possession of leased property after the lease has expired. The landlord agrees to the occupation by continuing to accept rent.

hollow-newel stair
A circular stairway having a hollow center. Usually the curve of the circle is severe.

hollow wall
A wall constructed of brick or stone which is actually two separate walls, joined only at the top and the ends, making it hollow. Also called a cavity wall.

holographic will
A will, written in the maker's own handwriting, dated, and signed by the maker. The will is not witnessed and is not recorded. It is generally not recommended as it may be easily contested.

home equity loan
A cash loan made against the equity in the borrower's home.

homeowners' association
A group of property owners in a condominium or other subdivision neighborhood, who manage common areas, collect dues, and establish property standards.

homeowners exemption
A $7,000 tax exemption available to all owner-occupied dwellings.

homeowner's insurance policy
Combined property and liability insurance designed for residential property owners.

homestead
A house and the surrounding land that is occupied as a home. In some states, homesteads are protected from judgments for debts in order to shield families from evictions. Both spouses must jointly execute any deeds conveying the homestead, further protecting each individual spouse's interest.

hood
A protective canopy extending over a door or window. Also used over a stove or oven to vent heat and fumes out of the building.

hospital window
A window that opens inwardly from bottom hinges with hoppers on its sides to prevent drafts.

hostile possession
Possession of real property by someone other than the rightful owner. Hostile means that the possessor's claim does not recognize, nor stand subordinate to, the owner's title. Hostile possession is necessary to establish a claim to real property under adverse possession.

hotel
A commercial establishment built solely for the purpose of accommodating travelers.

housekeeper
An employee in a hotel who cleans and stocks the guest rooms.

house zones
An appraisal term that refers to the different zones that make up the space in a house. The private-sleeping zone contains the bedrooms and bathrooms; the living-social zone refers to the living room, dining room, family room, and den; and the working-service zone includes the kitchen, laundry, pantry, and office. Circulation areas include the hallways, stairways, and entrances.

housing starts
The number of housing units currently under construction. Housing starts are often used as an economic indicator.

HUD
U.S. Department of Housing and Urban Development. HUD, created in 1965, administers the federal program dealing with better housing and urban renewal.

humidifier
A device that heats and vaporizes water for the purpose of adding moisture to the air, making it comfortable to breath.

HVAC (heating, ventilation, and air-conditioning)
A system that regulates the distribution of fresh air and heat throughout a building.

hybrid financing
The mixing of conventional forms of financing to create new loans such as participation loans and convertible loans. Hybrid financing counteracts weak real estate financial markets.

hypothecate
To pledge property as security for a debt without actually giving up possession or title.

I

IF (interest factor)
A theoretical rate of interest that is used to calculate the theoretical present or future worth of a sum of money or an annuity.

impact fees
Charges imposed by local governments on developers of new residential, commercial or industrial properties to compensate for the added costs of public services created by the new building.

implied contract
A contract created by acts and conduct rather than words.

implied agency
An agency created and performed without written agreement, but through words, actions, inference, and deduction from other facts.

implied listing
A listing agreement that is created by the actions of the parties involved, rather than by written contract. In some states, this type of contract is enforceable.

impound account
A trust account in which funds are held, usually by a lender, for the payment of property taxes and insurance premiums required to protect the lender's security. These amounts are usually collected with the note payment.

improvements
Structures, usually private, constructed on a property to facilitate its use and increase value.

improvement ratio
The value of the improvements divided by the total value of the property.

imputed interest
Interest that is applied by law. An interest rate imposed by the IRS, when the mortgage or land contract does not set one, or states one that is unreasonably low.

inclusionary zoning
Local zoning ordinances that require residential developers to include a certain percentage of units for low-income and moderate-income households. Compliance with these ordinances is a contingency for governmental approval of the building project.

income (capitalization) approach
The method by which the value of an income-producing property is estimated. The expected income from the property, over its remaining economic life, is capitalized.

income ratio
The difference between a borrower's total income and the amount necessary to cover one month's mortgage payment.

incompetent
A person who is legally unfit to enter into a contract. A person may be deemed incompetent by reason of mental illness, physical disability, drugs, age or other reason that causes them to lack sufficient understanding, or be incapable of making reasonable decisions.

increasing annuity
Regular, periodic payments that increase in amount.

indemnify
To protect against damage, loss, or injury, or to make compensation to for damage, loss, or injury.

independent contractor
A person who is hired to do a particular job and is subject to the control and direction of the person for whom they work. Independent contractors pay for their own expenses and taxes, and are not viewed as employees with benefits.

index
A statistical indicator that measures changes in the economy or in financial markets. The index is used to set interest rates, such as the six-month Treasury bill rate.

indirect lighting
A method of lighting by means of reflecting the light off the ceiling, wall, or other reflector, in order to soften glare.

individual retirement account (IRA)
An individual savings plan that provides income tax advantages to individuals saving money for retirement in an approved tax deferment program.

industrial development bond
A municipal bond that allows private investors to finance apartment and commercial developments by using tax-exempt, inexpensive funds. These bonds are issued by local governments to attract new businesses or help local businesses expand. They offer tax-exempt interest, but are generally considered risky.

industrial property
A property where products are manufactured or assembled.

industrial revenue bonds
Bonds issued to finance the construction of an industrial park or commercial building.

ingress
The way one enters a property; the opposite of egress.

inheritability
The right to will an estate to someone.

inheritance tax
A tax imposed on heirs who inherit property. The tax is determined not by the property inherited, but on the heirs for their right to acquire the property. As a result, the tax amount may vary depending on the relationship to the deceased.

innocent landowner defense
A legal defense used by an owner of property to avoid liability for environmental contamination. The defense may be used only if the property was acquired after the hazardous substance existed, and the owner did not know the contamination existed at the time he acquired the property. The owner must have taken certain measures to determine the environmental condition of the property prior to acquiring it.

in perpetuity
Of endless duration; forever.

inspection
A visit to, and review of, a particular site or building.

installment
The regular, periodic payments that a borrower agrees to pay a lender, in order to repay the loan.

installment sale
A sale in which the price is paid in installments. If the seller provides any sort of financing, it is considered an installment sale. A taxpayer may save on taxes by receiving smaller amounts over a period of years.

institutional lender
A financial institution such as a bank, insurance company, savings and loan association or other lending institution. These institutions receive money from depositors and customers, and then reinvest those deposits in mortgages. The government closely regulates institutional lenders in order to limit risk to investors.

instrument
A written, legal document setting forth the rights and liabilities of the parties involved.

insulation
Materials, such as fiberglass, rock wool, urethane foam, etc., which are used to slow heat loss and protect wires and other electricity carriers, and are placed in the walls, ceilings, or floors of a structure. Insulation comes in different forms: blanket, batt, rigid, fill, or reflective; and may be made of glass wool, cotton or wood fibers.

insurance
Policies that guarantee compensation to the policyholder in the event of loss from certain causes. Various forms of insurance exist to protect property owners from many types of risk, such as liability, flood, fire, etc.

intangible property
There are two categories of property; tangible and intangible. Tangible property is physical items such as equipment, land, buildings, and minerals. Intangible property is non-physical property such as copyrights, licenses, and the goodwill of a business. Intangible property also includes financial assets that represent value such as promissory notes, stock certificates, or certificates of deposit.

interest
In real estate finance, the cost of borrowing money. Also, a right or share of something; ownership that is incomplete or limited.

interest factor (IF)
A theoretical rate of interest that is used to calculate the theoretical present or future worth of a sum of money or an annuity.

interest only
A loan repayment plan in which monthly payments only go towards paying off the interest on the loan, and not to the capital. An investment or savings account is generally established to repay the capital at the end of the mortgage term.

interest rate
A percentage of a sum of money, charged for the use of that money, on a yearly or monthly basis.

interim financing
A short-term, interim loan usually made to finance the cost of construction. The loan money is disbursed in increments as construction progresses.

interim use
A short-term, temporary use of a property.

interior lot
A building lot that is surrounded by other lots, with a frontage on the street; the most common type of lot, which may or may not be desirable, depending on other factors.

intermediaries
Financial institutions such as banks, savings institutions, and life insurance companies.

intermediation
The process of transferring capital from those who invest funds to those who wish to borrow.

intestate
Dying without leaving a will.

intrinsic value
The value given to a geographical area or property based on its features and amenities, and an individual's personal preferences or choices. For example, a property located next to a shopping mall would most likely have a greater intrinsic value to someone than a property located next to a sewage treatment facility.

investment conduit
A means of investing. Examples include real estate trusts such as REITs, REMTs, and combination trusts.

investment property
Property, or an interest in property, that is purchased for the purpose of earning a profit.

investment value
The significance of a property to an investor.

involuntary lien
A lien imposed on a property as a consequence of a delinquency or failure to perform, such as a lien for delinquent taxes, a mechanic's lien or a judgment.

involuntary trust
A trust created when a person obtains title to property and/or takes possession of it and holds it for another, even though there is no formal trust document or agreement. The court may determine that the holder of the title holds it as a constructive trustee for the benefit of the intended owner. This may occur through fraud, breach of faith, ignorance or inadvertence. Also called constructive trust.

IRA (individual retirement account)
An individual savings plan that provides income tax advantages to individuals saving money for retirement in an approved tax deferment program.

J

Jacob's ladder
A hanging ladder, made with wooden steps and sides of rope.

jalousies
A series of louvers, or slats, used in doors, windows, shutters, etc., to keep out sun and rain, while letting in light and air.

jawboning
Pressure, although not force, applied by an authority, such as the Fed, to persuade its member banks to adhere to a policy. Also called moral suasion.

joint and several note
A loan for which two or more people or entities are creators, and are jointly and severally liable for repayment.

joint appraisal
An appraisal performed by more than one appraiser, but stating one common conclusion.

joint tenancy
Equal ownership of real estate, by two or more people, each of whom has an undivided interest, with the right of survivorship. Thus, the death of one joint tenant does not destroy the entity; the remaining joint tenants acquire the deceased person's interest.

joint venture
A business project by two or more persons by express or implied agreement. The partners have equal control, and share in profits and losses.

joist
A horizontal, parallel beam directly supporting the boards of a floor or the laths of a ceiling.

judgment
The final legal decision of a judge in a court of law regarding the legal rights of parties in a dispute.

judgment decree
An order by the court that specifies the award made in a civil case.

judgment lien
A general lien on a debtor's real and personal property. A judgment lien differs from a mortgage in that the lien is placed on all property owned by the debtor. The lien may be enforced by the sheriff seizing the property and selling it at auction to pay off the debt.

judicial foreclosure
Foreclosure by court action.

junior loan
A loan that has a subordinate or inferior priority to another loan.

junior mortgage
A second mortgage; one that is subordinate or has an inferior priority to the first mortgage.

junior trust deed
Any trust deed that is recorded after a first trust deed, and whose priority is less than the first.

just compensation
Fair and reasonable payment due a private property owner when his or her property is wholly or partially condemned under eminent domain.

K

Keogh plan
A tax-deferred retirement plan for self-employed individuals and unincorporated businesses. Also called a self-employed pension.

key lot
A potential building lot which resembles a key fitting into a lock; one that is surrounded by the backyards of other lots, and therefore is the least desirable because of the lack of privacy.

kicker
An additional feature, such as a bonus, which makes a loan more attractive to an investor or lender.

kiosk
A small structure, usually constructed with one or more sides open, often used as a newsstand or other small vending operation. The business occupying the kiosk often pays rent on a high percentage lease basis.

kite winder
The steps at the curvature of a circular stairway, which are triangular or kite-shaped.

L

laches
A legal doctrine that states that those who take too long to assert a legal right lose their entitlement to compensation. For example, Joe, knowing the correct property line, fails to bring a lawsuit to establish title to a portion of real estate until his neighbor, Jane has built a house that encroaches on the property in which Joe has title. Joe would not be entitled to compensation due to the doctrine of laches.

laissez-faire
A French term meaning "let do." A laissez-faire government does not interfere in economic or commercial affairs; a free market system.

land bank
Land that is purchased and held for future development. Also refers to the process of purchasing and holding land for future development. Scenic property is sometimes land banked to prevent its development in an effort to contain urban or suburban sprawl.

land contract
A contract for the sale of real property in which the seller gives up possession but retains the title until the purchase price is paid in full; also known as a contract of sale.

land description
A description of a piece of real property. The description may be legal and use a metes and bounds, recorded lot, block and tract system, or survey method to describe its location; or the description may be common, such as a street address. All deeds, mortgages, and sales contracts must contain a description of the land.

land projects
Subdivisions located in sparsely populated areas in California, made up of 50 parcels or more.

land residual method
A method of determining the value of land by calculating the net income of the land, less the value of any buildings on the land.

land trust
A trust created by the owner of real property in which the property is the only asset.

landlocked
A parcel of land that is without access to a public road.

landlord
Lessor; property owner.

land-use intensity
Local zoning codes that regulate the density of land development, including living space and recreation space requirements. Important considerations in the construction of planned unit developments.

large-lot zoning
Zoning used to reduce residential density by requiring large building lots. Also called acreage zoning or snob zoning.

late charge
An added fee a borrower is charged for failure to pay a regular loan installment when due.

lath
Material fastened to the rafters, ceiling joists or wall studs in the construction of a building to form a base for plaster, slates, tiles or shingles. Lath is usually made of wood, gypsum, wire or metal.

lawful object
A requirement of a valid contract. The purpose, object or action of a contract must be legal in order to make it valid.

late payment charge
A penalty fee charged for late payments.

lead poisoning
An illness caused by high concentrations of lead in the blood. Lead poisoning can cause major health problems, especially learning disabilities in children. Lead is commonly found in lead-based paint and water contaminated by lead pipes. By law, purchasers of houses built prior to 1978 must be given a lead disclosure form detailing the dangers of lead.

lease
An agreement to possess and use, for a finite period of time, real property, in exchange for rent. An estate for years, one form of a less-than-freehold estate.

lease concessions
Incentives offered to a tenant, by a landlord, in order to attract the tenant to sign a lease. The enticements may include the first month rent-free, or improvements made to the property at the landlord's expense.

leasehold
The right to use and possess property, for a finite period of time, created by a lease; a personal property interest.

leasehold lending
A loan in which a leasehold interest in a property is used as security or collateral. Some of these loans are eligible for FHA and DVA insurance.

leasehold mortgage
A mortgage loan in which a tenant's leasehold interest in a property is used as security or collateral.

lease option
A clause in a lease agreement that gives the tenant the option to purchase the property under certain conditions. The tenant may also have other options such as lease renewal or extension.

leasing agent
An agent who secures qualified tenants for leases on residential, commercial or industrial property.

legacy
A gift of personal property by will.

legal description
A standardized method of identifying a piece of land, using metes and bounds, lot and block, and/or the rectangular survey system.

legal notice
The legally required notification of others, as a result of property possession or document recordation. Legal notice may be a registered letter, advertisement in a designated newspaper, telegram or other such method. Also known as constructive notice.

legal title
Title that is complete and perfect.

legally permissible
One of the requirements in highest and best use analysis. For a use to be considered the highest and best, it must be legally permissible.

less-than-freehold estate
A leasehold estate, considered to exist for a definite period of time or successive periods of time until termination.

lessee
Tenant; renter.

lessor
Landlord; property owner

leverage
The utilization of borrowed funds to increase purchasing power, or using a smaller, borrowed investment to generate a larger rate of return.

liability
A financial obligation; a debt. Also a responsibility.

liability indemnity clause
A clause in a lease that holds a landlord harmless from the actions of his or her tenants.

license
Permission to use a property that may be revoked at any time.

licensee
A person who holds a valid real estate or appraisal license.

license laws
The laws that authorize states to license and regulate real estate brokers, salespeople, and appraisers. Many of these laws are based on the laws set forth by the National Association of REALTORS®.

lien
A form of encumbrance that holds property as security for the payment of a debt.

lien theory

One of two theories of mortgage security. Under a lien theory, the lender creates a lien on a borrower's real property, but the borrower retains the legal rights, as opposed to the lender gaining title to the property under a title theory. In the event of a loan default, the lender has no right of possession but must foreclose the lien and sell the property.

lien waiver

A legal document many property owners require contractors to sign, in order to protect their property. In signing the document, the supplier or contractor relinquishes their right to place a lien on the owner's property. The waiver is generally signed upon receipt of payment for the goods and services provided by the contractor.

life estate

An estate that is limited in duration to the life of its owner or the life of some other chosen person.

life tenant

A person whose interest in real property lasts as long as they (or some other person) live.

lifting clause

A provision included in a junior mortgage document that allows the underlying senior mortgage to be replaced or refinanced as long as the amount of the new senior loan does not exceed the amount of the first lien outstanding at the time the junior loan was made.

LIHTC (low income housing tax credit)

A tax credit given to owners for the construction or rehabilitation of low-income housing. To qualify for the credit, the property must be at least 20 percent occupied by individuals with incomes of 50 percent or less of the area median income, or be at least 40 percent occupied by individuals with incomes of 60 percent or less of the area median income.

like kind
In a real estate exchange, properties which are similar in nature or character. Improvements on land are considered to be differences in the quality of the property, but not in type. Thus, a bare lot may theoretically be exchanged fairly for an apartment house.

limited liability company (LLC)
A relatively new and flexible business ownership structure. Particularly popular with small businesses, the LLC offers its owners the advantage of limited personal liability (like a corporation) and a choice of how the business will be taxed. Partners can choose for the LLC to be taxed as a separate entity (again, like a corporation) or as a partnership-like entity in which profits are passed through to partners and taxed on their personal income tax returns. LLC's lack at least two of the following four characteristics: (1) continuity of life, (2) free transferability of interests, (3) centralized management, and (4) limited liability for equity investors.

limited partnership
A partnership comprising a general partner and limited partners. The general partner operates the partnership and is fully liable for the debts of the firm. The limited partners are merely investors, receive some of the profits, and have no influence in management. Their liabilities are limited to their original investment.

limited power of attorney
A power of attorney that is limited to a specific situation or job.

limiting conditions
In an appraisal report, conditions that restrict the assumptions contained in the report to certain situations. For example, the date and use of the appraisal.

line of credit
An amount that may be borrowed from a lender. The borrowed sum must be repaid in full on an agreed-upon regular date.

linear foot
A measurement meaning one foot or twelve inches in length as opposed to a square foot or a cubic foot.

line-of-sight easement
An easement that prohibits the use or modification of land within the easement area in any way that interferes with the view. For example, Joe has a line-of-sight easement over a portion of Fred's property that ensures him an unobstructed view of the nearby lake. Fred is thereby prohibited from building an addition on his house that blocks Joe's view.

linoleum
A durable, stiff floor covering used in heavy traffic areas such as kitchens, bathrooms, and entrances. It is made of cork, linseed oil, resins, and pigments on a canvas or burlap backing.

liquidated damages
An amount specified in advance of entering into an agreement that must be paid as a penalty in the event of a breach of the contract.

liquidation value
The price that a property could quickly be sold for, without reasonable market exposure, such as if a company were to go out of business and must be sold quickly to pay off debts.

liquidity
The amount of cash an individual, business or financial institution has on hand or readily available; the ability of an asset to be converted into cash quickly and without discounting the price.

lis pendens
A recorded notice that indicates pending litigation on a property, preventing a conveyance or any other transfer of ownership until the lawsuit is settled and the lis pendens removed.

listing
A property listed for sale with an agent. Also, the act of entering into a contract with an agent to sell a property.

listor
The real estate broker or salesperson who creates the listing agreement with a seller. Generally, the listor receives a percentage of the commission when the property sells. May also be spelled "lister."

littoral
Land bordering a lake, ocean, or sea; as opposed to land bordering a stream or river (riparian).

LLC (limited liability company)
A relatively new and flexible business ownership structure. Particularly popular with small businesses, the LLC offers its owners the advantage of limited personal liability (like a corporation) and a choice of how the business will be taxed. Partners can choose for the LLC to be taxed as a separate entity (again, like a corporation) or as a partnership-like entity in which profits are passed through to partners and taxed on their personal income tax returns. LLC's lack at least two of the following four characteristics: (1) continuity of life, (2) free transferability of interests, (3) centralized management, and (4) limited liability for equity investors.

loan constant
The annual mortgage payments divided by the mortgage balance. It is used to calculate the annual payment needed to pay off a loan.

loan-to-value ratio (LTV)
The ratio of the amount borrowed to the appraised value or sales price of a parcel of real property; generally expressed as a percentage.

loan transfer
The transfer to, or assumption of, existing financing by the new owner when a property is sold.

locational obsolescence
A type of external obsolescence in which value is lost due to its location. Examples are a corner lot location, nearby contamination or zoning changes near the property.

lockbox
A special locking box that the broker places on the door of a listed property. The keys to the property are placed inside the box, and a combination opens the box. This allows the listing broker access to the property, and other brokers may gain entry by calling the listing broker's office and obtaining the lockbox combination. Lockboxes are a way of securing the property, controlling entry, and facilitating its showing to prospective buyers.

lock-in clause
A clause in a loan agreement that prohibits repayment of the loan prior to a specified date.

loft building
A building with large un-partitioned floor areas often used for storage. They are also popular as contemporary residential units.

lord
In earlier times, a regional supervisor of a large piece of land.

lot and block system
A method of legal land description using tract, block, and lot numbers to identify a geographic area.

louver
The affixed or adjustable slats that make up a jalousie. The slats let in light and air, allow ventilation of fumes, yet keep out rain.

love and affection
The form of consideration used in a gift deed.

low income housing tax credit (LIHTC)
A tax credit given to owners for the construction or rehabilitation of low-income housing. To qualify for the credit, the property must be at least 20 percent occupied by individuals with incomes of 50 percent or less of the area median income, or be at least 40 percent occupied by individuals with incomes of 60 percent or less of the area median income.

low rise
A building with fewer than seven stories above ground level.

LTV (loan-to-value ratio)
The ratio of the amount borrowed to the appraised value or sales price of a parcel of real property; generally expressed as a percentage.

luminous ceiling
A type of ceiling emitting light from its entire surface, through the use of fluorescent light above translucent glass or plastic.

lump-sum contract
A construction contract in which the contractor agrees to perform a specific amount of work for a fixed price. The inflexible nature of the contract can create problems as well as advantages for the contractors and the employers.

M

maintenance
The general costs of operation and upkeep of a property, including employee wages, repairs, supplies, and services.

maintenance clause
A clause in a lease designating which party is responsible for maintenance of the property beyond normal wear-and-tear.

maintenance fee
An amount charged to property owners to maintain their property in an operational and productive state. This fee is charged especially to condominium owners.

maintenance supervisor
A position responsible for maintenance of buildings in his or her charge. This person hires workers and supervises all maintenance activities.

maker
The borrower who executes a promissory note and becomes primarily liable for payment to the lender.

management plan
A plan for future management that is based on financial reports and projection, and accepted by ownership.

mansard roof
A four-sided roof that slopes upward from the edge of the roof to a square peak. The roof has two different slopes around all sides of the structure, the upper of which may be nearly horizontal and the lower nearly vertical. An example of a mansard roof can be found on page 261.

mantel
The decorative facing around a fireplace. Mantels are usually constructed of wood or stone and topped with a shelf.

manufactured housing
A housing unit primarily constructed in a factory on a chassis and wheels, and designed for permanent or semi-attachment to land; also called a mobile home.

marble
A hard, single or multicolored limestone. In construction, it is used in place of tile in more expensive structures.

marketable title
Good or clear saleable title reasonably free from risk of litigation over possible defects.

market analysis
A study of the economic factors existing in and affecting the local marketplace that relates to the subject property.

market data approach
The method of estimating property value by comparing sale prices of comparable properties within the same area.

market indicators
Statistical measures of the construction and real estate industry, using industry activity such as number of permits issued, indices of building costs, deeds recorded, and homes for sale. Analysts use the indicators to forecast the market's direction.

market rent
The dollar amount the competition is receiving in rent for similar space with similar amenities. Used by property managers to set competitive rental rates.

market survey
A report generated by a property manager using computer software that compares the subject property in various categories of performance to competing properties in the area.

market value
The highest price a property is expected to bring under fair and normal market conditions.

masonry
Construction made from brick, cement block, or stone, which provides structural support as well as a decorative finish.

mass appraisal
The process of valuing an entire county market area. Neighborhoods, subdivisions, and large groupings of similar properties are appraised at one time.

master trust
A recorded deed of trust that contains general terms and provisions but names no specific parties and describes no property; it is used for reference only.

maturity
The date on which an agreement expires; the termination of a promissory note when the full amount is due.

maximally productive
One of the requirements of highest and best use. For a use to be considered highest and best, it must produce the highest value or price.

MBS (Mortgage Backed Security)
An investment instrument, a security, guaranteed by a mortgage pool. The securities are grouped together and sold to other institutions or the public; and investors receive a portion of the interest payments on the mortgages as well as the principal payments; usually guaranteed by the government.

mean
The average of a set of numbers. Mean is calculated by dividing the group's sum by the number of individual figures. For example, the mean of 4, 15, and 89 is 36 ([4 + 15 + 89] $\div$ 3 = 36).

measurement tables
A table of unit conversions from U.S. measurements to their metric equivalents.

mechanic's lien
A lien placed upon land or a building, as security for payment of labor and materials used to improve the property.

median
The middle figure in a numerically ordered set of figures. There are an equal number of values above the median as there are below. For example, the median of 4, 15, and 89 is 15.

meeting of the minds
Agreement between the parties in a contract situation. There can be no contract unless there is a meeting of the minds. A meeting of the minds may be enforceable if the actions and words of the parties indicate agreement.

mega-center
An oversized shopping center that may attract shoppers from hundreds of miles around. Also called a super-mall.

megalopolis
A large, densely-populated metropolitan area made up of several major urban areas.

menace
The illegal practice of using the threat of violence in order to get agreement in accepting a contract.

meridian
A survey line running north and south, used as a reference when mapping land.

metes and bounds
A method of land description in which the dimensions of the property are measured by distance and direction. Points along specific boundaries are used as references to measure the distances.

mezzanine
A small floor between two regular floors of a building.

MGIC (Mortgage Guaranty Insurance Corporation)
The nation's largest private mortgage insurance provider.

middle managers
Property managers who are involved in hands-on activities that implement the decisions and goals of owners and upper management.

mid-rise
A building with between 7 and 25 stories above ground level.

mile
A distance of 1,760 yards or 5,280 feet.

mill
One-tenth of one cent. In property tax assessment, the tax rate is expressed as a number of mills.

MIMO form
The move-in/move-out form; detailing inventory and initial condition of a rental space upon move-in, and inventory and condition upon move-out. The MIMO form helps to determine whether or not, and how much of, the rental deposit will be returned.

minimum lot size
The smallest dimensions allowed for a building lot, specified by zoning ordinance.

minor
Someone under 18 years of age, and thus, not of legal capacity to enter into any legal contract.

MIP (mortgage insurance premium)
A fee charged for either an FHA or private mortgage insurance policy; it may be a one-time payment at closing or included in the monthly payments.

misplaced improvement
An improvement on a piece of real estate whose highest and best use does not match that of the property.

misrepresentation
An innocent or negligent misstatement of a material fact causing someone loss or harm.

mission architecture
A Spanish style of architecture resembling those features of California missions.

mixed-use property
A property that may have more than one use. For example, a retail store with an apartment upstairs.

MLS (multiple listing service)
A marketing organization composed of member brokers who agree to share their listing agreements with one another in the hope of procuring ready, willing and able buyers for their properties more quickly than they could on their own. In exchange for a potentially larger audience of buyers, the brokers agree to share commissions. The service also provides members with information on mortgage loans, competitive market analysis data, and worksheets for qualifying buyers and estimating ownership and closing costs. The public can now obtain much of the information through various real estate websites.

mobile home
A housing unit primarily constructed in a factory on a chassis and wheels, and designed for permanent or semi-permanent attachment to land; also called a manufactured home.

mobile home loan
A mortgage loan made on a mobile home; usually created for a shorter period than a conventional real estate mortgage.

mode
The most frequent value in a set of numbers. If the set is very small, and there are no duplicate numbers, then there is no mode. For example, in 6, 7, 8, 6, 10, 12, and 14, the mode is 6. In 4, 6, 8, and 10, there is no mode.

molding
Long, narrow strips of wood or synthetic material, used as a finish piece to cover the crack where a wall meets a floor or ceiling. Used for decoration only.

monetary default
Defaulting on, or breaching the terms of, a loan by not making the agreed-upon payments.

money market certificate
A type of certificate of deposit or savings account in which a minimum balance is deposited and left alone until a specified date. The type of interest gained on that money is specific to the type of account and deposit. Most banks offer a wide variety of CD accounts that vary in the minimum investment and the length of time that they must sit before you can retrieve your deposit. A money market certificate requires a minimum investment of $2,000 and requires only 60 to 90 days before withdrawal.

money market fund
A type of mutual fund which is uninsured and unregulated.

monitor roof
A type of roof, usually used on industrial buildings, which has an elevated middle section to provide better ventilation and light.

month-to-month tenancy
A periodic tenancy in which no lease agreement exists, or where one has expired, and the tenant pays rent for one period at a time. The tenancy continues until either the lessor or lessee gives notice of termination, generally required at least one rental period in advance.

monument
A fixed landmark used in a metes and bounds land description.

moral suasion
Pressure, although not force, applied by an authority such as the Fed to persuade its member banks to adhere to a policy. Also called jawboning.

moratorium
A temporary prohibition against building in certain areas to control the rate of development.

mortar
A mixture of cement, an aggregate or sand, and lime and water in certain combinations. It is used to bind masonry units, such as brick, block or stone.

mortgage
The use of property as security for the payment of a debt; also, the document used to establish a mortgage lien.

Mortgage Backed Security (MBS)
An investment instrument, a security, guaranteed by a mortgage pool. The securities are grouped together and sold to other institutions or the public; investors receive a portion of the interest payments on the mortgages as well as the principal payments; usually guaranteed by the government.

mortgage banker
A banker who originates new mortgage loans, and services and sells existing loans in the secondary mortgage market.

mortgage broker
A banker who has access to many lenders and can locate and negotiate the best rates, terms, and conditions for borrowers, thereby earning a commission.

mortgage company
Businesses that lend money to individuals purchasing real or personal property.

mortgage constant
The sum of the annual mortgage payments divided by the mortgage balance. It is used to calculate the annual payment needed to pay off a loan.

Mortgage Guaranty Insurance Corporation (MGIC)
The nation's largest private mortgage insurance provider.

mortgage insurance premium (MIP)
A fee charged for either an FHA or private mortgage insurance policy; it may be a one-time payment at closing or included in the monthly payments.

mortgage lien
A lien or claim against a mortgaged property, created by the property owner, that secures the underlying debt obligations. The lien must be paid when the property is sold.

mortgage loan disclosure statement
A statement that informs the buyer of all charges and expenses related to a particular loan.

mortgage pool
A group of mortgages or other related financial instruments, combined for resale to investors on a secondary market.

mortgage release document
A document filed when a loan has been repaid in full, releasing the borrower of all obligations and the lender of all rights to the property.

mortgage revenue bond
A type of industrial development bond that is offered by state and local governments through their housing financing agencies. The interest rates are low and the bond is tax-exempt.

mortgagee
The lender under a mortgage.

mortgagee's title insurance
An insurance policy taken out by the lender to protect their investment in the case of a future default. As the loan is paid off, the insurance coverage is reduced. When the loan is fully repaid, the coverage terminates.

mortgagor
The borrower under a mortgage.

mortmain
The transfer of property to a church, school or charity. Mortmain statutes limit the percentage of an estate that may be transferred to such an institution.

motel
A hybrid of motor and hotel; a housing accommodation in outlying areas for middle-class America. Located along major highways, it gives easy access to lodging to those traveling by automobile.

motor camps
Chains of campgrounds designed to accommodate motorists and recreational vehicle drivers.

m roof
A type of roof formed by two double-pitched roofs, forming a shape similar to the letter M. These roofs utilize shorter rafters, making construction easier, and allow a lower overall height.

mud-jacking
The process of repairing a foundation, where cement grout is pumped through small holes, underneath the slab, in order to float the slab to a desired level.

mullion
A nonstructural, vertical strip separating the panes of a window or panels of a door. Also an upright framing member of panels or wainscoting.

multi-class mortgage securities
Short or long-term mortgage securities pooled together and sold to investors. The securities may or may not have pass-through privileges, or payments that are sent directly to investors.

multi-family units
Residential structures intended to house more than one family unit, such as duplexes or apartment buildings.

multiple listing agreement
A listing agreement created by a buyer with a real estate salesperson who is a member of a multiple listing organization in a particular area. In effect, it is an exclusive right to sell granted to the organization, but with the provision that the details of the listing will be circulated to other members of the organization. The listings are available on the Internet through various real estate sites, as well as distributed to all member salespeople in a periodic publication put out by the multiple listing organization.

multiple listing service (MLS)

A marketing organization composed of member brokers who agree to share their listing agreements with one another in the hope of procuring ready, willing and able buyers for their properties more quickly than they could on their own. In exchange for a potentially larger audience of buyers, the brokers agree to share commissions. The service also provides members with information on mortgage loans, competitive market analysis data, and worksheets for qualifying buyers and estimating ownership and closing costs. The public can now obtain much of the information through various real estate websites.

municipal bond

A county or state bond issued and sold in order to finance public improvements, such as schools, parks, and renewal projects.

municipal mortgage enhancement

An FNMA program used in multifamily development projects in which the most financially solid Fannie Mae mortgage-backed securities are exchanged for the underlying mortgage. This enables the developer to secure money at the lowest rate; commonly called "Munie Mae."

muntin

A nonstructural, horizontal strip that divides the panes in a window.

mutual consent

A meeting of the minds; both parties agreeing to the contract. One of the essentials of a valid contract.

mutual water company

A company that supplies water services in a particular area. The company may be organized by, or for, water users, and stock may be purchased by, and issued to, users.

N

naked legal title
Title ownership. One person may own naked legal title (the trustee) while another (the trustor) may have equitable ownership (possession).

NALP (National Apartment Leasing Professional)
A designation offered by the National Apartment Association (NAA).

NAR (National Association of REALTORS®)
The largest and most prestigious real estate organization in the world. It is made up of local boards and state associations, and only members may use the trademark REALTOR®. Members must adhere to a strict Code of Ethics.

narrative report
A type of appraisal report that does not have a structured form. It includes an introduction, assumptions of the appraisal, presentation and analysis of data, and addenda.

National Apartment Leasing Professional (NALP)
A designation offered by the National Apartment Association (NAA).

National Association of REALTORS® (NAR)
The largest and most prestigious real estate organization. It is made up of local boards and state associations, and only members may use the trademark REALTOR®. Members must adhere to a strict Code of Ethics.

National Environmental Policy Act (NEPA)
A law passed by Congress in 1970 that requires an environmental impact statement to be prepared and released prior to any federal action that would affect the environment. This is also required by some state and local governments for private improvements.

natural finish
A finish that retains the color and appearance of the original surface. An example is varnish applied to wood.

negative amortization
Negative amortization occurs when the monthly payments on a loan are insufficient to pay the interest accruing on the principal balance. The unpaid interest is added to the remaining principal due.

negative easement
An easement that prevents a landowner from using or improving the land in a certain way. Examples of negative easements are building restrictions and view easements.

negotiable instrument
Any written instrument that may be transferred by endorsement or delivery.

negotiation
The act of bargaining in order to reach a meeting of the minds between parties in a business transaction. Negotiation is a necessary part of the real estate sales process.

neighborhood barrier
Any natural or man-made features that separate one neighborhood from another.

neighborhood center
A retail center supported by about a thousand households, usually anchored by a grocery store and supported by a dozen other stores.

NEPA (National Environmental Policy Act)
A law passed by Congress in 1970 that requires an environmental impact statement to be prepared and released prior to any federal action that would affect the environment. This is also required by some state and local governments for private improvements.

net annual income
The amount of income left from an income-producing property after all expenses have been deducted. Also called net operating income.

net effective rent
The net income derived from a lease after deducting all costs incurred by the landlord for procuring the lease, such as leasehold improvement allowances, real estate fees, free rent, etc. The resulting figure is generally expressed as an annual dollar amount per square foot.

net income
The amount remaining after expenses are deducted from gross income.

net lease
A lease which requires the tenant to pay rent as well as part or all of the taxes, insurance, repairs, and other ownership expenses. Also known as triple net lease or absolute net lease.

net listing
A listing agreement in which the broker receives all the money received from the sale of a property, in excess of the minimum sales price agreed to by the broker and seller. Such a listing agreement is discouraged in most states, and is illegal is some, because of the high danger of unethical practices.

net operating income
The amount of income left from an income-producing property after all expenses have been deducted. Also called net annual income.

net rate
The rate of interest given to an investor after servicing fees have been deducted from the gross rate.

net realization value
The amount of profit from the sale of a property, after all transaction expenses are paid.

net rentable area
The actual square footage of a building that can be rented. Areas such as hallways, lobbies, and elevators are excluded.

net worth
An individual or company's total assets, less their total liabilities. Net worth is often used to determine creditworthiness and financial health.

neutral depository
A third party, generally an escrow company, which holds the documents and funds related to a real estate transaction until the conditions of the agreement are fulfilled. The neutral depository becomes the trustee for the money and papers until they are distributed according to the escrow instructions.

newel
The post around which a circular stairway is constructed. In a noncircular stairway, the major post at the bottom of the stairway or at a landing.

no brokers involved
A disclosure statement included in some escrow instructions when there are no brokers involved in the transaction, no deposit receipt has been written, and no commissions will be paid. The statement, when initialed by buyer and seller, indicates acknowledgment of the arrangement.

nominal rate
The agreed-upon interest rate of a loan, adjusted for inflation. Also called the contract rate.

nonconforming
A property whose use was legal according to the zoning requirements at the time of construction, which is allowed to remain even though zoning has changed, technically making the current property use illegal.

nonfiduciary
Refers to certain lenders who provide funds for real estate finance. They owe no duty to others and can maintain complete discretion over their activities because they invest their own funds. Nonfiduciaries include title insurance companies, private loan companies, and individuals.

nonjudicial foreclosure
The power to foreclose on a property without court approval. Also called a strict foreclosure or forfeiture.

non-monetary default
A loan default that is the result of something other than non-payment. The default comes from failure to perform some other condition of the loan agreement.

nonprofit corporation
A corporation formed for a purpose other than making a profit. Examples include charities, as well as political and educational organizations. These corporations do not have shareholders, but are controlled and maintained by a board of directors.

nosing
The front edge of a step that projects over the riser below.

notary public
A public officer who is authorized to function as an official witness to contracts, administer oaths, take acknowledgments of deeds and other conveyances, and to perform other official acts. If the person has a beneficial interest in a document, he or she may not act as a notary public to that document.

no tax advice
A disclosure statement included in escrow instructions stating that buyer and seller have not received any tax advice from either agent.

note
A loan document that is signed by the borrower and serves as evidence of the debt. The document states the loan amount, the terms of the loan, the interest rate, the obligation to repay, and method of repayment.

notice
An announcement of an event or fact. Notice may be written or oral. Most contracts contain a paragraph that defines proper notice and tells the parties how to give notice.

notice of default
A notice to a defaulting party that they have not paid their debt.

notice of delinquency
When junior and senior loans exist, the borrower may authorize the senior lender to send a notice to the junior lender in the event of a default.

notice of lien
A written notice of the creation of a mechanic's lien; required in some states. A copy of the notice must be served to the owner and other parties involved.

notice of trustee's sale
Notice that a trustee's sale will be held to sell a property in order to satisfy a debt.

notice to quit
A step in the eviction process. A written notice given by a landlord to a tenant, stating that the landlord intends to retake possession of the property and that the tenant must leave. The notice may indicate whether the tenant must vacate at the end of the lease term, or earlier.

notorious possession
Open and active possession of a property. The possession must be so open (notorious) that the owner is presumed to know of it and its extent. One of the requirements for adverse possession.

novation
The substitution of a new obligation for an old one.

nuisance
A land use that is incompatible or that interferes with surrounding land uses. Examples are land uses that create loud noise or pollution in a residential area. Nuisances may be avoided through private deed restrictions and zoning laws.

O

obligor
A promisor; someone who establishes a legal obligation to another. One example of an obligor is someone who creates a promissory note.

observed depreciation
The decrease in a building's utility that results in a loss of value. Depreciation that is identified through physical inspection.

obsolescence
The cause of depreciation in a property. Obsolescence may be external, such as zoning changes, or functional, such as a structural defect.

occupancy agreement
An agreement that permits the buyer to occupy the property before the close of escrow, in exchange for rent paid to the seller. Such an agreement should be in writing.

offer
A presentation or proposal to form a contract.

offer and acceptance
Two elements of a valid contract.

offeree
The party receiving an offer.

offeror
The party making an offer.

office classifications
A method of rating office buildings used by appraisers. Their rating is based on location, physical condition, and potential financial returns.

Class A:	Excellent location and access, building is in excellent physical condition, meeting or exceeding building codes, and returns are competitive with new construction.
Class B:	Good location, building is in good condition and meets building codes, but suffers some functional obsolescence or physical deterioration, and rents are below new construction.

office classifications (cont'd.)

Class C: Building is 15-25 years old and may not meet building codes, it suffers physical deterioration and functional obsolescence, has reasonable occupancy rates at lower rents.

Office of Thrift Supervision (OTS)

The primary regulator of all federally chartered and many state chartered thrift institutions, which include savings banks and savings and loan associations. OTS is funded by assessments and fees levied on the institutions it regulates.

offsite improvements

Improvements that are made outside the property's boundary line, such as the installation of streets, sidewalks, and sewers.

on-site manager

A property manager who lives on-site, handles day-to-day activities, and interacts with tenants on a regular basis.

open beam construction

A construction design using heavy roof beams as interior decoration. The beams are exposed to give a roomy appearance.

open bid

A real estate transaction where the bids are accessible to all potential buyers. In open bidding, the potential buyers know what other bidders have offered, and can alter their bid accordingly. The sellers can also see the bids as they are presented and choose or negotiate the best one. Most real estate sales are open bid transactions.

open end loan

A loan that is expandable by increments up to a certain amount. The total amount is secured by the same mortgage.

open house
A house that is open to prospective buyers or tenants for inspection during certain hours and days of the week, without an appointment.

open listing
A listing agreement that gives any number of brokers the right to sell a property. The first broker to obtain a buyer earns the commission. Unlike an exclusive listing agreement, an open listing does not necessarily require a specific termination date. Contractors and builders often use open listing agreements.

open market operations
The buying and selling of government securities by the Fed in the open market in order to increase or decrease the amount of money in the banking system.

open space
Land that has not been improved or built upon. Often left open by a developer for recreational use.

open valley
A style of roofing where valley flashing is left uncovered by shingles. Water flows from the shingles to the valley and is directed off the roof.

operating budget
An itemized statement of income, expenses, net operating income before debt service, and cash flow. A basic tool of the property manager to help in planning for future operation. The operating budget gives the property owner an idea of the cash yield expected from the property during a period of time, generally a typical year.

operating expenses
Expenditures necessary to the operation of an income-producing building, such as employee salaries. Operating expenses are subtracted from effective gross income to arrive at net operating income.

opportunity cost
The cost of choosing one alternative over another. The potential income from one investment that must be sacrificed when another investment is chosen instead.

option
A right to purchase or lease property at a future time. The option holder is not obligated to exercise the right.

oral contract
A contract made verbally. Real estate and lease contracts should not be oral; they should be written to avoid conflict and misunderstandings.

ordinance
A law adopted by a local governing body. Typically, local governments issue ordinances establishing land usage and parking rules; ordinances also regulate noise, garbage removal, and the operation of parks and other areas that affect people who live or do business in the area.

oriel window
A window projecting outward, similar to a bay window. However, unlike a bay window, that is supported by the foundation, an oriel window is supported by brackets or a cantilever.

origination fee
The fee charged by a lender for creating a mortgage. The fee is generally a percentage of the total loan amount and covers initial costs such as preparation of documents, credit fees, inspection fees, and appraisal fees.

"or more" clause
A clause in a promissory note that allows a borrower to pay it off early with no penalty.

ostensible agency
An agency relationship that is created by the actions of the parties, instead of verbal or written agreement.

OTS (Office of Thrift Supervision)
The primary regulator of all federally chartered and many state-chartered thrift institutions, which include savings banks and savings and loan associations. OTS is funded by assessments and fees levied on the institutions it regulates.

overage
The rent paid in addition to the fixed base rent. Overage is usually based on an index or percent of sales. It is usually discounted at a higher rate because it is less certain than the fixed base rent.

overhang
An extension of a roof beyond the exterior walls, used as shading or protection from rain.

overriding trust deed
A method of financing in which a new loan is created that includes both the unpaid principal balance of the first loan and whatever new sums are loaned by the lender. The new loan is placed in a secondary position to the original loan. Also called an All-Inclusive Trust Deed (AITD).

ownership, form of
Any one of many ways to own property. Determining the type of property ownership may affect which kinds of documents that must be signed during a property transaction as well as affecting future rights to the property. A broker should have extensive knowledge and understanding of the different forms of ownership and their accompanying rights. Examples of different forms of ownership are tenancy by the entirety, tenancy in common, tenancy in severalty, joint tenancy, community property, partnership trust, and corporate forms of ownership.

owner's title insurance
An insurance policy taken out by the buyer in order to protect themselves for the amount of a property's purchase price in the event of a future title dispute.

P

package loan
A loan on real property that can be secured by land, structure, fixtures, and other personal property.

page
An employee in a hotel who delivers a message or summons a guest.

paired sales analysis
An appraisal method of valuation, matching up two properties that are identical in all respects except for one variable. This type of analysis determines the value of that variable in the marketplace. For example, two properties in the same neighborhood are identical in size, age, and amenities. The only difference is one has a swimming pool in the back yard. The difference in sales price between the two properties indicates the value of the swimming pool in that particular marketplace.

PAM (pledged account mortgage)
A type of loan under which a sum of cash paid by the owner is set aside in an account. The account is drawn upon during the initial years of the loan to supplement periodic mortgage payments. This reduces the payment amounts in early years.

pane
The glass portion of a door or window.

panic peddling
Making written or verbal statements that cause fear or alarm in order to gain sales or rental listings. Panic peddling is often associated with sales or rentals to minorities. It is illegal.

par
A term used to refer to the face value of a bond or security.

parapet
A short wall along the edge of a roof or terrace to protect the edge and divert rainwater.

parole evidence rule
In a dispute over a real estate transaction, the parole evidence rule refers to any evidence that is not written. Thus, any agreement between buyer and seller, made prior to, or outside of, the written sales contract is inadmissible.

parquet floor
A floor constructed with short pieces of hardwood laid in various patterns, as opposed to a strip floor in which the pieces are laid end to end.

partial eviction
A situation in which a landlord's negligence renders a portion of the property unusable to a tenant.

partial release
A provision included in a mortgage agreement that allows some of the mortgaged property to be released from the mortgage contract if certain conditions are met, such as when a certain amount of the mortgage is repaid.

partially amortized installment note
A promissory note with a repayment schedule that is not sufficient to pay off the loan over its term. At maturity, the remaining principal balance is due in full.

participating broker
A brokerage company or one of its agents who finds a buyer for a property that is listed with a different brokerage company. The brokers generally split the commission 50-50. A participating broker may also be a broker who simply assists the listing broker, whether or not the broker is an agent of any of the parties involved in the transaction.

participation financing
Financing in which the lender is also a partner. This enhances the profitability and safety of the lender's position in the arrangement.

participation loan
A large loan created by more than one lender, thus enabling the borrower to obtain more financing than from an individual lender; a loan in which the lender receives partial ownership in the financed project.

partition action
A court action to divide a property held by co-owners.

partnership
Two or more people who act as co-owners in a business. Title to real property may be held by the partnership, in the partnership's name.

party wall
A wall that is shared by two separate parcels of property. The owners of both properties simultaneously use and maintain the shared wall.

pass-through
The proceeds from the sale of securities in the secondary market that are passed on to the securities buyer.

patent deed
Deeds used by the United States government when confirming or transferring ownership to private parties.

payoff
The final payment of a debt.

payoff letter
A statement, issued by a lender, showing the unpaid principal balance, accrued interest, outstanding late charges, legal fees, and all other amounts necessary to pay off a debt in full.

PCAM (Professional Community Association Manager)
An advanced designation offered by the Community Associations Institute (CAI).

pension plan
A retirement plan funded fully or in large part by an employer. Many pension plans are being replaced by 401k plans.

penthouse
A condominium or apartment on the roof of a building that is used as a residence. Also, a small building on a rooftop which houses elevator machinery, ventilating equipment, etc.

percentage lease
A lease on a commercial property, whose rent is determined by a base amount, plus a percentage of the tenant's gross sales.

percolation test
A test performed by a hydraulic engineer to determine the ability of soil to absorb water. This information is crucial to determining the amount of development an area can sustain.

perfect escrow
An escrow in which all the necessary documents, money, and instructions are in the escrow agent's possession.

perfecting title
The process of eliminating any claims, flaws or defects affecting a title.

performing loan
A loan that has and continues to, fulfill all of the terms and conditions required under the mortgage.

period hotel or inn
A hotel or inn that conveys the essence of a particular period of time in history.

periodic tenancy
A form of tenancy in which no lease agreement exists, or where one has expired, and the tenant pays rent for one period at a time. The tenancy continues until either the lessor or lessee gives notice of termination, generally required at least one rental period in advance. An example of periodic tenancy is month-to-month tenancy.

permanent financing
A long-term loan ranging from 20 to 30 years with fixed or variable interest rates.

personal income
An individual's gross income from all sources.

personal property
Tangible and movable items not permanently attached to property that do not transfer to the buyer in a transaction, unless otherwise stipulated in the agreement.

personal property included in price
A section of escrow instructions, identifying personal property that is included in the property's price, and which will be transferred to the buyer in the transaction.

PHA (Public Housing Authority)
Local public agency under the control of HUD that administers HUD's Low-Income Public Housing Program and other HUD programs.

physical deterioration
The loss of value or utility by disintegration of physical condition due to wear and tear and/or neglect. It may be curable or incurable.

physical life
The period of time a structure is considered habitable or physically useful.

physically possible
One of the four criteria for determining highest and best use. For a use to be considered the highest and best, the size, shape, and terrain of the property must be able to accommodate the use.

picture window
A large window that cannot be opened. It is used to let in light and a view, but not air.

pier and beam foundation
A type of foundation using piers which rest on footing support beams or girders, which in turn support the superstructure. It is a relatively inexpensive form of foundation, rarely used for residential homes.

piers
Columns designed to support a concentrated load. Pier columns are made of steel, steel reinforced concrete or wood, and transfer the building load to the ground.

pilaster
A pier or column, which partly protrudes from a wall, or is attached to a wall as a decoration. It is usually decorative, but it may also be a support member.

piling
A vertical support piece of a structure, driven into the ground, which supports the foundation.

pillar
A vertical support member, usually the main support, unattached at its sides.

placement fee
A fee charged by a mortgage broker for bringing together a borrower and a lender who subsequently negotiate a loan agreement.

Planned Unit Development (PUD)
A development in which each owner owns his or her own housing unit and land, and has an undivided interest in common areas with other owners. Designed to produce a high density of dwellings and maximum use of open spaces. PUDs are an efficient use of land, allowing greater flexibility for residential land and development.

plaster of Paris
A type of gypsum cement in the form of a white powder that forms a paste when mixed with water and hardens into a solid; used in making molds and sculptures and casts for broken limbs.

plat map
A surveyor's map of land, showing natural and man-made boundaries, buildings and other improvements.

platform framing
A type of construction framing in which the building is constructed one story at a time so that each story serves as a platform for the next. Platform is the most common type of framing.

pledge
The transfer of property to a lender to be held as security for repayment of a debt.

pledged account mortgage (PAM)
A type of loan under which a sum of cash paid by the owner is set aside in an account. The account is drawn upon during the initial years of the loan to supplement periodic mortgage payments. This reduces the payment amounts in early years.

plottage
The increase in value when two or more contiguous properties are joined together and made available as a single unit. Also called assemblage.

plumbing system
The system of pipes and fixtures for the distribution of clean water and the disposal of sewage in a building.

plywood
Wood made of three or more layers, or plies, of veneer joined with glue, usually laid with the grain of adjoining plies at right angles to one another. This arrangement makes plywood strong and highly resistant to movement from expansion and contraction.

PMM (Purchase Money Mortgage)
A mortgage that is used as partial payment for a property. A purchase money mortgage is usually used when the buyer is unable to borrow commercially for the purchase price.

points
A factor used in rate adjustment. One point is equal to 1 percent of the principal conventional loan amount. Points are a one-time charge paid for the use of money.

police power
The government's right to impose and enforce laws in the interest of public safety and welfare.

porte cochere
A roofed structure that extends from the entrance of a building to a driveway offering shelter to people getting into or out of vehicles.

porter
A baggage handler in a hotel.

portfolio manager
An executive who oversees a firm's real estate resources, and sets goals and strategies with ownership interests. Also called an asset manager.

portico
A grand porch or entrance to a building that is supported by columns and often covered.

possession
Possessing or occupying property, whether actually or constructively. Actual possession is physically occupying the land; constructive possession is legally possessing title to a property.

post-house
An inn accommodating travelers in the 1600s.

potable water
Water that is fit to drink, according to water standards established by the Public Health Service.

potential gross income
The total potential income of which a property is capable, during a specific period of time.

power of attorney
A written instrument giving a person legal authority to act on behalf of another person.

power of sale
A clause in a trust deed or mortgage that gives the holder the right to sell the property in the event of default by the borrower.

pre-approved loan
A pending loan in which all the necessary documents and information have been filed, and there appears to be no credit or income issues to prevent the loan from being approved and granted. It does not necessarily mean the lender will actually grant the loan.

preliminary title report
An examination of the public land records to determine the extent to which someone has legal interest in a parcel; a report on the quality of the title that searches for encumbrances and liens or any other items of record that might affect ownership; used as a basis for title insurance.

premium
A fee paid for an insurance policy, paid in one lump sum, or in monthly installments.

premium in excess of par
The price paid for a security in excess of its face value.

prenuptial agreement
An agreement made between a man and woman before they wed, establishing property rights of each during the marriage, and in the event of their divorce or a death. Also called an antenuptial agreement.

prepaid interest
Interest charged on a loan that is paid before it is incurred.

prepayment
The payment of all or part of a debt before it is due. There are sometimes penalties associated with prepayment.

prepayment clause
A clause in a trust deed that allows a lender to collect a certain percentage of a loan as a penalty for an early payoff.

prepayment penalty
A penalty charged to a debtor if they repay a loan before it matures. The penalty is charged so the lender can recover some of the interest they would have been paid if the loan was allowed to mature.

prepayment privilege
The right given to a borrower to repay all or part of a mortgage debt prior to its maturity, without penalty.

pre-qualified loan
A loan that is pending and, based on a preliminary interview and a credit report, whose requirements it appears the borrower will be able to meet – assuming the borrower is telling the truth about his or her financial situation and income status.

pre-tax cash flow
The portion of net operating income after debt service is paid, but before income tax is deducted. Also called before-tax cash flow or equity dividend.

prescription
The acquisition of an interest, or a right to use property through long, uninterrupted possession. Examples include an easement or right of way. Similar to adverse possession; however, one acquires title to property through adverse possession. Adverse possession also requires the payment of property taxes, where prescription does not.

present worth
The value of today's money, projected into the future. Using a mathematical equation that factors the amount of money, the interest rate per period, and the number of periods, the future value of today's money may be calculated.

price
The amount of money, or other consideration, paid for a specific good or service.

primary interest rate
The minimum interest rate charged by lenders on loans made to borrowers with the best credit rating. Also called the prime rate.

primary lenders
Originators of real estate loans.

primary mortgage market
The market in which lenders originate loans for borrowers, usually service the loans, and bear the long-term financing risk.

prime rate
The minimum interest rate charged by lenders on loans made to borrowers with the best credit rating. Also called primary interest rate.

principal
Someone who directs or authorizes another to act in his or her place regarding relations with third persons. The buyer or seller. Also, the amount of money borrowed; the original amount borrowed.

principal meridian
North-south running lines used by surveyors to establish and define legal land descriptions.

priority lien position
The order liens appear on public record. Priority generally follows the order of recording. However, real property tax liens have priority over recorded liens, regardless of their date of recording.

private grant
The granting of private property to other private persons.

private mortgage insurance (PMI)
Mortgage insurance issued by private companies.

probate
When someone dies, probate is the official process by which the will is validated or proven. The estate's assets are collected, all debts and taxes are settled or paid, and the heirs or those who stand to inherit are identified.

probate sale
A court-approved sale of the property of a deceased person.

Professional Community Association Manager (PCAM)
An advanced designation offered by the Community Associations Institute (CAI).

proffer
To offer an opinion or advice up for approval.

profit and loss statement
A document containing a detailed summary of the income and expenses of a business. It shows the financial health of a business over a certain period of time. Also referred to as a "P&L," "operating statement," or "income statement."

pro-forma statement
A financial statement of the future income and operating expenses of a real estate property based on a certain set of assumptions. A pro-forma is used to create budgets and determine economic feasibility.

progression
An appraisal concept referring to the increase in value of a lower-end property caused by its proximity to higher-end properties. It is the opposite of the principle of regression.

project operating report
A report that breaks income and expenses down into specific categories and matches them to budget objectives.

projection
An anticipated operational income and expense statement projected into the future to aid in planning.

promissory note
A written promise or order to pay at a future specified time; evidence of a debt.

property
Something owned; any tangible or intangible possession that is owned by someone. May be real or personal.

property analysis
An on-site inspection and study of the subject property so that the entire physical plant is thoroughly understood.

property management
The practice of real estate that manages, leases, markets, and preserves the real property of another person.

property supervisor
A property manager who is responsible for several properties and supervises the on-site managers of those properties.

property tax
Tax that is charged on either real or personal property. Only the state and local governments have the constitutional right to tax land. In most states, the general property tax becomes a lien on January 1, with payment of the tax due sometime later in the year.

Proposition 13
A California referendum that limits the amount of annual property tax increases.

prorate
To divide, distribute, or assess proportionately.

prorations
Rents, taxes, interest, payments on bonds and assessments assumed by buyer, homeowners fees, and other expenses of the property that are divided or distributed between buyer and seller at the closing.

prospect
A potential buyer or seller in a real estate transaction. A prospect does not become a client until a fiduciary relationship is established, most often by signing a listing or sales contract.

prosperity
A stage in the business cycle when unemployment is low and consumers have strong purchasing power.

proxy
The power or authority to act for another. The written document giving a person authority to act for another. Also refers to the person authorized to act for another.

p-trap
A plumbing device, used to prevent sewer gas from entering a building, by keeping a water seal in the drain. A P-trap uses a vertical inlet and a horizontal outlet to accomplish this seal.

public accommodation property
A privately owned property where the public has certain rights, such as a hotel or office building.

public dedication
The giving of private property for public use.

public grant
The transfer of title by the government to a private individual.

Public Housing Authority (PHA)
Local public agency under the control of HUD that administers HUD's Low-Income Public Housing Program and other HUD programs.

PUD (Planned Unit Development)
Each owner owns his or her own housing unit and land, and has an undivided interest in common areas with other owners. Designed to produce a high density of dwellings and maximum use of open spaces. PUDs are an efficient use of land, allowing greater flexibility for residential land and development.

puffing
Exaggerated comments or statements made by a real estate salesperson about a property, not as representations of fact, but as an innocent way to encourage a sale, thus not grounds for misrepresentation.

purchase agreement
A written agreement between a buyer and seller, detailing the price and terms of the purchase.

Purchase Money Mortgage (PMM)
A mortgage that is used as partial payment for a property. A purchase money mortgage is usually used when the buyer is unable to borrow commercially for the purchase price.

purlin
A horizontal structural member of a building, running at right angles to the rafters that is used as support between rafter end points.

pyramid roof
A roof with four sloping sides that rise to a ridge. Usually found on garages or church steeples. Also called a hip roof. You can see a diagram of a pyramid, or hip, roof on page 261.

pyramiding through refinancing
A method of acquiring additional properties through refinancing of existing mortgages, then reinvesting the proceeds in new property.

Q

qualified buyer
A buyer who is financially capable of paying the asking price for a property. Some buyers are pre-qualified by a lender before submitting an offer to buy property.

quantity survey method
A method of estimating building costs by calculating the cost of all of the physical components of the construction, adding the cost of the labor to assemble them, plus insurance, taxes, etc. Also called "price take-off" method.

quiet enjoyment
The right of a tenant to be undisturbed.

quiet title action
A lawsuit to establish or settle title to real property, and thus "quiet" any challenges or clear any clouds on the title. A quiet title action generally occurs when there is some question or problem with the title recording, property description, or easement discrepancy. It is also used by adverse possessors to substantiate the title.

quitclaim deed
An instrument that transfers only that interest in the property in which the grantor has title. Quitclaim deeds are commonly used by married people seeking a divorce. Usually one spouse signs all his/her rights to the real estate over to the other. Quitclaim deeds are also used to clear up questions of full title when a person has a possible but unknown interest in the property. Quitclaim deeds do not warrant good title.

R

radiant heat
Heat transmitted by radiation as opposed to heat transmitted by conduction or convection.

radiation
The flow of energy across open space via electromagnetic waves such as light and heat.

radon
Naturally occurring, colorless, odorless, radioactive gas that seeps up from the ground into some homes, through sump pumps, or cracks in the foundation; it is considered a health hazard.

rafter
Any of the beams that slope from the ridge of a roof to the eaves to serve as support for the roof.

ranch style house
Commonly used to describe any one-story house. However, a true ranch style house is rambling, with low-pitched gable roofs, and with an open, airy interior design.

random shingles
Roof or siding shingles of different sizes.

range
A land description used in the U.S. Government Survey system consisting of a strip of land, measuring six miles wide, running north and south.

rate
The percentage of interest charged on the loan principal.

ratification
The approval of a previously authorized act, performed on behalf of a person, which makes the act valid and legally binding.

"ready, willing, and able"
A phrase that refers to a prospective buyer's legal capacity and financial ability to purchase property. A broker may earn a commission when they find a "ready, willing and able" buyer, regardless of whether the seller actually goes through with the sale.

real estate
Real property; the land, and all things attached to it, including air rights and subsurface rights.

real estate agent
Someone licensed by the Department of Real Estate, holding either a broker or salesperson license, who negotiates sales for other people.

real estate broker
Someone permitted by law to employ real estate salespeople and who may also negotiate sales.

real estate cycle
The cycle of supply and demand in real estate that is affected by the business cycle. The changing cycle results in changes in the level of activity for building, lending, purchasing, and leasing real estate. The cycle swings between the extremes of a buyer's market and a seller's market.

Real Estate Investment Trust (REIT)
Investors who individually possess a small amount of capital, pool their resources to buy real estate.

real estate law
The law that affects the licensing and conduct of real estate agents.

Real Estate Mortgage Investment Conduit (REMIC)
A tax entity created by the Tax Reform Act of 1986 that issues multiple classes of investor interests (securities) backed by a pool of mortgages. It avoids the double taxation generally imposed on similar corporations.

Real Estate Mortgage Trust (REMT)
A type of REIT that buys and sells real estate mortgages, rather than the real estate itself.

real estate sales associate
The same as a real estate salesperson, holding a real estate license, and employed by a broker.

real estate salesperson
Someone holding a real estate license and employed by a real estate broker, for pay, to perform any of the activities of a real estate broker.

Real Estate Settlement Procedures Act (RESPA)
A 1974 federal law that requires disclosure of mortgage loan settlement costs to both the buyer and seller.

real property
Land, anything affixed to the land, anything appurtenant to the land, and/or anything immovable by law. Also, the bundle of rights and interest of ownership in real estate.

Real Property Administrator (RPA)
The most widely used designation in the asset and property management fields. It applies to overall property management and administration. The designation is offered by the Building Owners and Managers Institute (BOMI). Candidates must pass a series of courses, including an ethics course, and have at least three years of previous property management experience.

real property sales contract
An agreement to purchase real property for a certain price and under certain conditions. Usually, the buyer makes a down payment and pays the rest in installments over a period of time. The buyer usually gains possession of the property, but takes title only when the purchase price has been paid in full.

realized capital gains
Investment profits that are not subject to income tax, such as profits from refinancing, exchanges, and installment sales.

REALTOR®
The registered trade name that may be used only by members of the National Association of REALTORS® (NAR). The designation indicates a salesperson who adheres to the strict Code of Ethics, and the rules and regulations adopted by the NAR.

recapture rate
The rate at which invested capital is returned to the investor, from a "wasting asset," or one that is depreciating.

recasting
The act of redesigning an existing loan balance in order to avoid a default. The loan period may be extended, payments reduced, or the interest rate periodically adjusted to help the distressed borrower.

receiver
An impartial person appointed by the court to manage properties that are involved in foreclosure or other litigation. The receiver collects the property's rents and profits, and applies or disposes of them as directed by the court.

recession
A stage in the business cycle when production and supply surpasses demand, resulting in unemployment and declining prices.

reciprocal easements
Easements created as covenants to limit the use of the land for the benefit of all the owners in an entire tract. Typically at the site of a planned subdivision.

recognition clause
A clause included in a blanket loan contract used to purchase a tract of land for subdivision and development. It protects the rights of buyers of small parcels in case of default by the developer.

recognized capital gain
Profits from the sale of investments that are subject to income tax. The figure is derived by subtracting the adjusted book basis from the net proceeds of the sale.

reconciliation
The final calculation of all the information of value gathered about a property during an appraisal in order to estimate the market value.

reconveyance
The act of transferring title of property back to the original owner. In the case of a deed of trust, the borrower conveys title to a third-party trustee as security for the debt. When the debt is paid off, the property is reconveyed to the owner.

reconveyance deed
A deed that is issued to convey the property back to the original owner, once the mortgage is repaid.

recording
The act of filing with the county recorder the written documents affecting the title to real property, such as deeds, mortgages, contracts for sale, options, and assignments.

recovery
A stage in the business cycle following a recession when consumers once again buy goods at reduced prices, increasing demand in relation to supply.

recovery fund
A fund used to compensate individuals who have suffered losses due to fraudulent acts or misrepresentation by a real estate licensee. The fund is created and maintained with fees paid by real estate licensees as part of their registration process with the state.

rectangular survey method
A method of legal land description using east-west lines (base lines) and north-south lines (principal meridians). Additional lines are drawn six miles apart and are known as township lines (east-west) and range lines (north-south). Also called the government survey method.

redemption period
The time period, following a foreclosure, during which mortgagors may buy back their foreclosed properties by paying the balance owed on their delinquent mortgages, plus interest and fees.

red flag
A warning. Something that indicates a potential problem and deserves further investigation. A broker would consider a water-stained ceiling a red flag of a possible roof-leakage problem.

redlining
The practice whereby mortgage lenders figuratively draw a red line around minority neighborhoods and refuse to make mortgage loans available inside the red lined area. It is a form of discrimination and illegal under Fair Housing law.

referral
The recommendation to a prospective client of a specific salesperson. Also, a client who is obtained through the recommendation of another. A referral fee may be due to the referring broker.

refinancing
Creating a new loan, usually at a lower interest rate, to pay off an existing loan, using the same property as security.

refrigerant
Fluid used in cooling systems that absorbs heat, changing into a vapor in the process.

regional center
A large retail shopping center (sometimes called a mall) with half a dozen major department stores along with 100 to 200 general merchandise and specialty shops. Customers are drawn from as far as 50 miles and comprise 50,000 to 150,000 households.

regional manager
A property manager who works for a large property management company and oversees the work of property supervisors or on-site managers.

registered bond
A bond issued to a specific owner; it can be transferred only if endorsed by the owner.

Registered Property Manager (RPM)
A property management designation offered by the International Real Estate Institute (IREI).

regression
An appraisal concept referring to the decrease in value of a higher-end property caused by its proximity to lower-end properties. It is the opposite of the principle of progression.

Regulation Z (Truth-in-Lending Act)
A truth-in-lending provision enacted in 1969 that requires lenders to inform borrowers about the cost of borrowing money, so that they may make informed choices from whom to borrow their money

reinforcing bar
Steel bars that are placed in concrete slabs, foundations, footings, piers, etc., to provide reinforcement. Also called rebar.

reinstate
To bring current and restore.

REIT (Real Estate Investment Trust)
Investors possessing a small amount of capital and who pool their resources to buy more real estate than would be possible individually.

release clause
A provision in a mortgage allowing for the release of part of a property from the mortgage after a proportional amount of the mortgage has been paid.

release of liability
An agreement that releases the borrower from obligation for repayment of a loan.

reliction
The exposing of previously covered land by receding water.

relief valve
A valve that is set to open at a certain pressure level to prevent the pressure in a container or system from reaching unsafe levels; used in plumbing systems.

remainder estate
Occurs when one grant simultaneously creates two or more estates. One estate does not take effect until the termination of the other estate. For example, Bob owns a property that he conveys to Joe, and upon Joe's death, the property shall go to Alice. Alice holds a remainder estate in the property.

remainderman
An individual who is entitled to take a remainder estate sometime in the future.

remaining economic life
The amount of time an improvement is expected to continue to add value to the land.

remediation
The removal of contaminants from a building or land.

REMIC (Real Estate Mortgage Investment Conduit)
A tax entity created by the Tax Reform Act of 1986 that issues multiple classes of investor interests (securities) backed by a pool of mortgages. It escapes the double taxation generally imposed on similar corporations.

REMT (Real Estate Mortgage Trust)
A type of REIT that buys and sells real estate mortgages, rather than the real estate itself.

renegotiable rate mortgage
A mortgage with an interest rate that can be modified by the lender at specified intervals (e.g., three or five years). Usually the increase or decrease must remain within a specified range and may be tied to an index. Also known as an adjustable rate mortgage.

rent
Payment for the use of a property, generally under a lease agreement.

rent back by seller
The practice of renting back property for a period of time, from the buyers, after the close of escrow. For example, if the sellers have not found another place to live, they may rent the property they just sold, until they secure a new residence.

rent control
A local ordinance prohibiting rent increases on certain types of property.

rent-up
The requirement of a lender, that the developer prove a certain percentage of the commercial space will be rented. The developer may have to do this in order to obtain financing, and the percentage required usually represents the rental income needed to break even.

repairs
Alterations and improvements made to a property to maintain its condition or restore it to its original condition. Repairs are made to extend the useful life of the property.

replacement cost
The estimated cost to replace a structure, using current construction costs.

reproduction cost
The estimated cost to replicate a structure, using current construction costs.

request for notice
A request for notice to be sent to any parties interested in a trust deed, informing them of a default.

rescission
Legal action taken to repeal a contract either by mutual consent of the parties or by one party when the other party has breached a contract.

reserve requirements
The amount of money and liquid assets the Federal Reserve requires member banks to set aside as a safety measure. The amount is usually a percentage of deposits.

reserves
A portion of earnings, assets or deposits that businesses and banks set aside to cover any losses or withdrawals.

residential property
A property where people reside, including single-family residences, condominiums, and apartment buildings.

resolution trust corporation (RTC)
The federal agency in charge of managing and liquidating the assets of failed savings and loan associations.

RESPA (Real Estate Settlement Procedures Act)
A 1974 federal law that requires disclosure of mortgage loan settlement costs to both the buyer and seller.

restriction
A limit on how property may be used. Private restrictions are created by covenants, conditions, and restrictions, or "CC&Rs," that are written into leases and deeds. Public restrictions are created by zoning ordinances.

restrictive covenant
A clause in a deed or lease that restricts the way the property may be used or occupied. The restriction runs with the land and normally restricts things such as lot size, building lines, type of architecture, and land uses.

retaliatory eviction
An eviction that occurs in retaliation for some complaint made by the tenant.

retrofit
A modification performed on a building to incorporate changes made after construction.

return on investment (ROI)
The income derived from an investment in one year. Usually expressed as a percentage of the total amount invested.

revenue bonds
Public improvement bonds that are paid for by the revenue generated by making the improvements for which the bonds are issued.

reverse annuity mortgage
A loan that enables elderly homeowners to borrow against the equity in their homes by receiving monthly payments from a lender, that are needed to help meet living costs.

reversion
A provision in a conveyance stating that the land will return to the grantor upon the occurrence of an event or contingency (often upon the death of the person to whom the property is being conveyed). The right of a lessor, upon termination of a lease, to possess the leased property.

reversionary right
The right reserved by a landlord, when granting possession to a tenant, to retake possession of the property after the lease term has expired.

reversionary value
The estimated value of a property at the expiration of a certain time period.

revocation
The canceling of an offer to contract by the person making the original offer.

revoke
To recall and make void.

RevPAR
Revenue per available room; the amount of income actually made, compared with how much income is possible, if every available room were rented. A statistic followed in the lodging industry.

rezoning
A change or amendment made to the zoning in a geographic area.

ridgeboard

The highest horizontal member of a roof, running along the ridge, and meeting the rafters at right angles.

right of first refusal

The right of a person to have the first opportunity to purchase or lease real property. The holder of the right cannot exercise the right to purchase until the owner actually offers the property for sale or entertains an offer to purchase from a third party. If the holder of the right decides not to exercise his/her right, then the owner is free to accept the offer made by the third party or any other party at that price or higher.

right of survivorship

One of the characteristics of joint tenancy. If one of the joint tenants dies, the surviving joint tenants automatically acquire an equal portion of the deceased joint tenant's right, title, and interest. The death does not destroy the joint tenancy.

right-of-way

The right to use or pass over a certain portion of another's property. The right may be acquired by contract or by accepted usage. A right-of-way may be either private, as in an access easement given a neighbor; or public, as in the right of the public to use the highways or streets or have safe access to public beaches.

riparian rights

The rights of a landowner whose land borders a river, stream or other watercourse, including the right of access, use, flow, and drainage. As opposed to littoral rights, which are rights associated to land bordering non-flowing water such as a lake, ocean or sea.

risk manager

A property manager who evaluates and attends to complex issues in order to protect the value of real estate assets.

rod

A length measuring the equivalent of 5 ½ yards or 16 ½ feet.

ROI (return on investment)
The income derived from an investment in one year. Usually expressed as a percentage of the total amount invested.

rollover mortgage
A loan that allows the rewriting of a new loan at the termination of a prior loan.

rotunda
A room or building, shaped in a circle, usually with a domed roof.

row houses
A method of construction of individual houses with common side walls and a common roof. Also referred to as townhouses.

RPA (Real Property Administrator)
The most widely used designation in the asset and property management fields. It applies to overall property management and administration. The designation is offered by the Building Owners and Managers Institute (BOMI). The candidates must pass a series of courses, including an ethics course, and have at least three years of previous property management experience.

RPM (Registered Property Manager)
A property management designation offered by the International Real Estate Institute (IREI).

RTC (Resolution Trust Corporation)
Established by the Federal Government in 1989, the RTC helps failed savings and loans liquidate real property assets.

running with the land
The transferring of rights or covenants affecting property to successive owners. For example, restrictive building covenants in a recorded deed affecting all future owners of the property.

S

safe rate of interest
An interest rate provided by relatively low-risk investments such as high-grade bonds or well-secured first mortgages.

SAIF (Savings Association Insurance Fund)
The fund that insures deposits made to savings and loan institutions.

sale-buyback
A financing arrangement in which an investor buys property from a developer, and immediately sells it back under a long-term sales agreement wherein the investor retains legal title.

sale-leaseback
A financing term referring to a property owner who sells the property to an investor or lender, while simultaneously leasing it back. This practice is generally used with commercial property in order to access capital that would otherwise be tied up in the property.

sales contract
A contract for the sale and purchase of real property. The buyer agrees to purchase the property at a certain price and the seller agrees to convey the title under certain conditions.

salesperson
A person who is employed by a licensed real estate broker to perform a variety of acts in the business of real estate. Salespeople may either be employees of, or independent contractors to, a broker.

sales tax
An amount charged to consumers when purchasing certain products. A percentage of the proceeds collected by the retailer are forwarded to the State Board of Equalization, an independent agency that hears and decides upon appeals of property valuations and classifications.

sandwich lease
A lease agreement created when a tenant sublets the property to another person, thus creating a sublessor-sublessee relationship. The person in the "sandwich" is a lessee to the owner and a lessor to the sub-lessee.

satisfaction
Full payment of a debt.

savings and loans
A banking and lending institution created by state or federal government. By law, a percentage of their loans must be home mortgages.

Savings Association Insurance Fund (SAIF)
The fund that insures deposits made to savings and loan institutions.

saw-tooth roof
A series of single-pitched roofs, resembling the sharp edge of a saw. Usually used in factories, this roof contains windows in each facing to allow maximum lighting. Not used in modern construction.

scenic easement
An easement created to preserve a property in its natural state and prevent its development.

Scheduled Gross Income (SGI)
All of the income a property is scheduled to produce.

second trust deed
The evidence of a debt that is recorded after a first trust deed; a junior trust deed.

secondary financing
A loan that is subordinate to a primary loan and cannot be satisfied until the primary loan is paid. Most governmental loan programs permit secondary financing, but place restrictions on its use.

secondary mortgage market
The place where primary mortgage lenders sell the mortgages they make to obtain more funds to originate more new loans. It provides liquidity for the lenders.

second mortgage
A mortgage that is subordinate to a primary mortgage. A secondary mortgage is generally created when the borrower needs additional money. Because greater financial risk is involved with a second mortgage, the borrower may be subject to more stringent conditions.

section
An area of land, as used in the government survey method of land description; a land area of one square mile, or 640 acres. It is 1/36 of a township.

Section 8 program
One program of the U.S. Department of Housing and Urban Development (HUD). The Section 8 program subsidizes the rent of low- and moderate-income tenants.

Section 1031, Internal Revenue Code
A section of the Internal Revenue Code that permits exchanges of like-kinds of property in order to postpone payment of income taxes on some capital gains. The properties must be held for business use or as an investment.

securitization
The pooling of traditional bank assets, loans, mortgages or other non-tradeable financial transactions, and converting them into tradeable securities.

security
Something deposited or given as assurance for the fulfillment of an obligation; a pledge.

security deposit
Money given to a landlord to prepay for any damage that might occur to a property, during a lease term, beyond normal wear and tear. Most states require landlords to hold the money in a separate account and refund the amount, or some portion thereof, if limited or no damage is done.

seller's market
A stage in the real estate market in which demand is greater than supply (more buyers than sellers) and prices rise.

seller's permit
A permit that allows a retailer to buy his or her product at wholesale prices without paying sales tax. The retailer must then collect the proper sales tax from customers and pay it to the State Board of Equalization, an independent agency that hears and decides upon appeals of property valuations and classifications.

semicircular roof
A roof resembling an extended arch. Usually found on barns or barracks type buildings.

semifiduciary
A general source of funds for financing real estate transactions, such as a mortgage broker or banker, a trust, a bond dealer or an endowment fund manager. It is different from a fiduciary as it is not a first-person relationship. This allows the semifiduciary to take more risks than the primary financial fiduciary.

senior loan
A real estate loan that has first priority.

septic system
An underground, self-contained sewage treatment system that has a storage tank where waste is decomposed through bacterial action. Septic systems are usually used in rural areas without sanitary sewer systems.

septic tank
A watertight sewage collection tank, located beneath the ground, where waste is decomposed through bacterial action. It is part of a septic system, which processes the waste and distributes it to the absorption field.

sequester of rents
When the rental income from a property is ordered by the court to be deposited with, and held by, the clerk of the court or other governmental/court official. Usually as payment for a debt.

serfdom
In medieval times, a social status that was subservient to the king and insufficient to allow a person to own land.

service of process
The official act of notifying a defendant of an upcoming lawsuit, and the delivery of his or her summons. Service is usually performed by the sheriff.

servicing fee/rate
The fee earned by a servicer for administering a loan for an investor; usually expressed as a percentage of the unpaid principal balance of the loan and deducted from the monthly mortgage payment.

servient tenement
The property that is burdened by an easement.

servitude
A burden on a property. The servitude benefits one owner who enjoys the use of a neighboring property. A servitude runs with the land. An example of a servitude is an easement.

setback
A zoning restriction that determines the distance a house or building must be from the lot line.

settlement
The paying, or prorating of all the credits, charges, and costs associated with a real estate transaction. Also, in a lawsuit, coming to an agreement or compromise.

severalty
Ownership of real property by one person or entity. The owner's title is severed from any other person.

SFR (single family residence)
A building that is designed for, and occupied by, one family. It is the opposite of a condominium, apartment or PUD. The definition of "family" varies by ordinance.

SGI (Scheduled Gross Income)
All of the income a property is scheduled or expected to produce.

shake
A thick wooden shingle, hand cut from logs, used for roofing or siding.

Shared Appreciation Mortgage (SAM)
A mortgage in which the lender and borrower agree to share a certain percentage of the increase in market value of the property.

sheathing
Sheets of material (plywood) that are applied across floors, rafters or studs to form the first layer of an outer wall.

sheriff's deed
A deed given to a buyer when property is sold through court action in order to satisfy a judgment for money or foreclosure of a mortgage.

shingle
A thin, wedge shaped piece of material, such as fiberglass, slate, cedar, asphalt, etc., that is used as a weatherproofing cover for roofs or as siding.

shoring
The use of timbers to prevent the sliding of earth at a construction site.

short circuit
A malfunction of the electrical wiring that results in a portion of the current being diverted to a conductor that is not the usual part of the circuit. This causes overheating and subsequent burnout.

short sale
A sale of encumbered real property that produces less money than is owed to the lender. The lender essentially decides to cut his or her losses and releases the property from the mortgage or trust deed so it can be sold free and clear. An alternative to foreclosure. Lenders may prefer short selling because they may be able to recoup more of their investment than foreclosing. For example, Mary purchased a home in 1990 for $190,000, and she now owes the bank $170,000. She must sell the house and move, but due to the economic downturn, she can only get $145,000 for it. Mary must either pay the bank the $25,000 difference at closing, or apply for a short pay-off, in which the bank will forgive the $25,000. Applicants must prove they are forced to sell due to financial hardship. Also called a short pay-off or short pay.

siding
Any variety of materials used as final covering on the exterior of a house. Materials such as aluminum or vinyl siding eliminate the need for repeated painting.

sight glass
A glass window in the liquid line of a refrigerant system that allows one to see if there are vapor bubbles in the liquid refrigerant line.

signature
A mark or name upon a document or instrument, in order to make it valid. In real estate, to be acceptable for recordation, a signature generally must be in black ink and be one's full legal name.

signs
Any printed displays used to advertise the availability of real estate. The REALTOR® Code of Ethics states that signs should be placed on listed property only with the consent of the owner.

silo
A tall, cylindrical structure, usually used to store grain.

simple interest
Interest that is charged only to the principal loan amount outstanding.

single family residence (SFR)
A building that is designed for, and occupied by, one family. It is the opposite of a condominium, apartment or PUD. The definition of "family" varies by ordinance.

single net lease
An arrangement whereby the tenant pays the rent plus utilities, property taxes, and any special assessments on the property.

single pitch roof
A roof pitched entirely at the same angle, usually over 20 degrees.

sinking fund
A fund established to hold money in preparation for a future debt.

site
A plot of land that has been improved or is deemed suitable for building.

skylight
A roof window that allows natural light into a room. Certain types of skylights can be opened and closed to provide ventilation.

skyscraper
Tall steel-framed structures that originally housed mostly offices, but now may also serve as private residences or hotels.

slope
The degree to which a piece of land deviates from level. It may be expressed in degrees of an angle, as a ratio of vertical rise to horizontal run or as a decimal.

SMA (Systems Maintenance Administrator)
A property management designation offered by the Building Owners and Managers Institute (BOMI) with emphasis on supervision of systems and personnel.

SMT (Systems Maintenance Technician)
A property management designation offered by the Building Owners and Managers Institute (BOMI) with emphasis on the technical maintenance of various systems such as heating and air conditioning.

snob zoning
Zoning used to reduce residential density by requiring large building lots. Also called acreage zoning or large-lot zoning.

soffit
The external area under the roof overhang, or the covering over the space under the eaves of a structure, frequently with an opening for attic ventilation.

soil
The upper layer of ground that supports plant life.

Soldier's and Sailor's Relief Act
A federal law designed to protect persons in the military service from loss of property when they are unable to make payments due to their military service.

SOP (Standard Operating Procedures)
Procedures that have been established to increase efficiency whenever specified regularly occurring events take place.

Spanish architecture
An architectural style that copies the houses of Spain and Mexico. Usually the homes have a courtyard, tiled roof, and are usually constructed of adobe or stucco.

special assessment
Any special charge levied against real property for public improvements (e.g., sidewalks, sewers, etc.) that benefit the assessed property.

special purpose properties
Properties with unique and limited purposes within a community, such as mini-storage facilities, churches, and schools.

Special Studies Zone Act
A disclosure statement in California escrow documents confirming that the buyer is aware that the subject property is located in a Special Studies Zone, and that construction or improvement of any structure may require the submission of a geological report by the buyer, prepared by a registered geologist. A Special Studies Zone is an area along a potentially hazardous fault line in which development is limited.

specific lien
A lien placed on a specific property of the debtor, rather than a general lien placed on all properties.

specific performance
A court action brought about by one party to force the other (breaching) party to fulfill the conditions of the contract. Specific performance is an alternative to a judgment for money. For example, if a seller was contracted to deliver the property on a certain date and failed to do so, the buyer may sue for specific performance to force the seller to turn over the property.

split-fee financing
A type of financing in which the lender purchases the property, leases it to the developer, and finances any improvements. The lender receives a basic rental rate from the developer, plus a percentage of the profits.

split financing
A method of real estate financing in which land and improvements are financed separately. Often used by developers to obtain more financing than would be available with conventional financing.

square-foot cost
A method for calculating the reproduction cost of a building by multiplying the number of square feet by the square-foot cost of a recently built comparable structure.

split-level
A house in which two or more of the levels are constructed directly above one another, and one or more additional floors are adjacent to them and constructed at a different level.

Standard Operating Procedures (SOP)
Procedures that have been established to increase efficiency whenever specified, regularly occurring events take place.

standard policy
A policy of title insurance covering only matters of record. It does not cover against clouds that are off-record, such as encroachments, unrecorded easements, and boundary-line discrepancies.

standby commitment
A promise by a lender to fund a long-term loan in order to buy out, or take out, the construction lender once the building is successfully completed.

standby takeout commitment
A promise by an interim lender to advance money to buy out, or take out, the construction lender. A form of interim financing.

statute of frauds
A state law that requires certain contracts to be in writing and signed in order to be valid and enforceable. In real estate, the final agreement must be in writing, but preliminary agreements and negotiations may be oral.

statute of limitations
A statute limiting the period of time during which legal action may be taken on a certain issue. The statute attempts to protect against outdated claims about which truth and justice may be difficult to determine.

statutory
Laws created by the enactment of legislation as opposed to laws created by court decisions.

statutory redemption period
A limited period of time in which a debtor whose property has been foreclosed upon and sold may repay the debt and regain their property.

steering
The illegal practice of directing people to specific locations for housing accommodations, depriving them of choice. Steering is a violation of Fair Housing Laws.

step-down annuity
A type of annuity in which payments are level until a specific date, and then decrease to a specified amount where they remain until the next adjustment.

step-up annuity
A type of annuity in which payments are level until a specific date, and then increase to a specified amount where they remain until the next adjustment.

step-up lease
Sometimes called a graduated lease; usually a long-term lease with smaller payments in the beginning, and "stepped-up" or larger payments upon the occurrence of a certain event or passage of a period of time.

stigmatized property
A property considered undesirable because of events that occurred there such as murder, gang activity, or proximity to a nuclear plant. A real estate broker may be required by state law to disclose certain types of stigmas associated with the property.

stock cooperative
A development in which a corporation is formed for the purpose of holding title to improved real property.

stop date
The date on which a term loan's balloon payment is due.

storm sash (storm window)
An extra window on the outside of an existing window, as additional protection against cold weather.

straight-line depreciation
The reduction in value of a property, in annual, equal increments. It is used in accounting for replacement and tax purposes.

straight-line method
An appraisal method of computing accrued depreciation. It assumes that a building depreciates at a fixed rate over the course of its life. The depreciation is then calculated by dividing the total economic life by its current effective age. Also called the age-life method.

straight note
A promissory note in which payments of only interest are made periodically during the term of the note, with the principal payment due in one lump sum upon maturity; it may also be a note with no payments on either principal or interest until the entire sum is due.

straw man
One who purchases property for another in order to conceal the identity of the true purchaser.

strict foreclosure/forfeiture
A foreclosure proceeding in which the debtor has a limited amount of time, once appropriate notice has been given, to repay the debt before their equitable and statutory redemption rights are waived and full legal title to the property is granted to the lender. This type of foreclosure is rarely used in contemporary markets.

strip center
A small retail center located in the suburbs, containing half-a-dozen to a dozen stores of various kinds.

stucco
A wet plaster finish, specifically designed for exterior use. Stucco is very popular as an outside wall surface in warm, dry areas.

subagent
An agent's agent. An agent of a person who is already acting as an agent for a principal.

Subdivided Lands Law
A law in some states that protects purchasers of property in new subdivisions from fraud, misrepresentation or deceit in the marketing of subdivided property.

subdivision
A plot of land divided into smaller portions for the purpose of building.

Subdivision Map Act
A California state law that established rules for filing maps when developing a subdivision.

subjective distance
The perceived distance between two points. Consumers perceive the distance and travel time to be different than they are in reality. Pleasant circumstances can make subjective distance shorter, while unpleasant circumstances can make it longer.

"subject-to" clause
A clause in escrow documents which states that the buyer will take over payments on an existing loan, but assumes no personal liability for the loan.

sublease
A lease that transfers all or part of a property to another, with the original lessee remaining liable for the original rental agreement.

subletting
The process by which an original tenant gives up use or possession of all or part of the property to another, but receives payment from the sub-lessee and remains fully responsible for the entire lease payment to the landlord.

subordinate lien
A lien or encumbrance on a property whose priority is inferior to another claim's on the same property.

subordination agreement
An agreement in which the holder of a superior mortgage agrees to give up priority to an existing or impending lien. Subordination agreements make an exception to the rule that gives priority to the mortgage that is recorded first. They are often used in development projects.

subordination clause
A clause in a contract in which the holder of a trust deed permits a subsequent loan to take priority.

subrogation
The adoption of a person's legal rights whose debts or expenses you have paid. For example, you pay off someone's debt and then try to get the money from the debtor yourself. Subrogation occurs when an insurance company pays off its injured claimant, takes the legal rights the claimant has against the third party that caused the injury, and sues that third party.

substitution, principle of
The appraisal method that states the value of a subject property is influenced by the cost of acquiring a comparable, or substitute, property.

substructure
In construction, the structural support materials of a building usually located underground. Examples include piers, footings, beams and slabs.

suburban hotel
A lodging accommodation within driving distance of the downtown area of a large city, designed to attract business clientele.

suburbs
The area within reasonable driving distance of a city's downtown.

succession
The legal transfer of a person's interest in real and personal property to their named heirs or beneficiaries under the laws of descent.

suction line
Tubing or piping in a refrigeration system that carries gas from the evaporator to the condenser.

summation
A method of determining the capitalization rate in which various risk factors are weighted and combined.

sump
A pit built into the basement of a building that allows for the drainage of excess water and moisture in order to avoid or minimize flooding.

superadequacy
A type of functional obsolescence caused by a structural component that is too large or of a higher quality than what is needed for the highest and best use of the property. An item whose cost exceeds its value.

superfund
Officially known as the Comprehensive Environmental Response, Compensation and Liability Act (CERCLA), passed by Congress in 1980. It established two trust funds to help finance the cleanup of properties that have been impacted by the release of hazardous wastes and substances.

superintendent of service
The person in a hotel who supervises all front office service personnel.

superior lien
A lien or encumbrance on real property whose priority is greater (or superior) to another's claim on the same property.

super-mall
An oversized shopping center that attracts shoppers from hundreds of miles around. Also called a mega-center.

supply and demand, principle of
A basic economic principle in which the greater the supply of an item, the lower its value. When an item is scarce in relation to demand, the value is high. The value of a property will increase as demand increases, and/or supply decreases.

surface skimmer
A device used in swimming pools that is located in the pool wall and is used to clear debris from the surface of the water. The skimmer draws water through a weir, or barrier, catching debris while releasing clean water back into the pool.

surrender
The voluntary giving up of a lease.

suspend
To temporarily make ineffective.

swale
A wide, shallow depression in the ground designed to channel rainwater off of property.

sweat equity
The value added to a property due to physical work done by the owner, such as do-it-yourself improvements.

swimming pool
A constructed or prefabricated pool of water, generally used for recreational swimming. The pool is usually at least 18" deep.

swing loan
A short-term loan that allows a buyer to purchase property before selling, and receiving the money from, another. Also called a bridge loan or gap loan.

syndicate
A group of individuals who come together for the accomplishment of some business purpose. Examples include corporations or limited partnerships.

Systems Maintenance Administrator (SMA)
A property management designation offered by the Building Owners and Managers Institute (BOMI) with emphasis on supervision of systems and personnel.

Systems Maintenance Technician (SMT)
A property management designation offered by the Building Owners and Managers Institute (BOMI) with emphasis on the technical maintenance of various systems such as heating and air conditioning.

T

t-intersection lot
A lot that is fronted head-on by a street; noise, and glare from car headlights may be detractors from this type of lot.

takeout financing
Long-term, permanent financing. Takeout financing is most often used in large construction projects. The developer generally first obtains a short-term loan to cover construction costs, but then signs a permanent loan to "take out" the short-term loan.

tandem plan
An investment plan that provides low-interest rate mortgages to low-income, qualified buyers. The Federal National Mortgage Association (FNMA) purchases low interest rate mortgages at a discount from the Government National Mortgage Association (GNMA).

tangible property
There are two categories of property; tangible and intangible. Tangible property is physical items such as equipment, land, buildings, and minerals. Intangible property is non-physical property such as copyrights, licenses, and the goodwill of a business. Intangible property also includes financial assets that represent value such as promissory notes, stock certificates, or certificates of deposit

tax deed
A deed given to a successful bidder at a tax auction.

tax-exempt bonds
Bonds issued to finance public or private improvements. The interest derived from the bonds may be exempt from federal, state, and local income taxes.

tax-free gifts
Gifts that are free from federal gift taxes. The gifts may be up to $10,000 annually from each donor to each recipient.

tax-increment financing
Financing established to stimulate community growth and generate increased tax revenue. State and local industrial development boards arrange the financing.

tax lien
A lien imposed on property for nonpayment of taxes. A tax lien remains with the property until the taxes are paid, even if the property is conveyed to another person.

Tax Reform Act of 1986 (TRA '86)

Legislation enacted in 1986 that drastically revised income tax laws, lowered tax rates, and eliminated many tax shelters.

Tax Relief Act of 1997

A law enacted in 1997 that decreased the capital gains tax rate, thereby decreasing the high taxes charged to people after selling their investment or personal property.

tax roll

A list of all taxable property showing the assessed value of each parcel; it establishes the tax base. Also called an assessment roll.

tax sale

The sale of real property by the government to pay off real property tax liens. There is usually a mandatory redemption period following the sale.

tax shelter

A strategy or technique of reducing income tax liability.

tenancy at will

A written or oral agreement, allowing a tenant to use or occupy property with the permission of the owner. The term of the tenancy is unspecified and the tenant may leave at any time, or at the request of the owner.

tenancy by the entirety (entireties)

A special joint tenancy by a husband and wife in which they hold title together and in the event of one spouse's death, the surviving spouse becomes the owner of the entire property.

tenancy for life

A life estate. The term of the estate is limited to the lifetime of the grantee or other specified individual.

tenancy for years
A tenancy created by a lease for a fixed period of time. If the tenancy is for more than one year, the agreement should be in writing.

tenancy in common
Ownership of property by two or more persons, each of whom has an undivided interest, without the right of survivorship. Upon the death of one of the tenants, that ownership share is inherited by the heirs or beneficiaries named in the decedent's will.

tenancy in partnership
Ownership by two or more persons who form a partnership for business purposes. Each partner has an equal right of possession. Upon the death of one of the partners, that partner's interest transfers to the remaining partner(s).

tenancy in severalty
Ownership of property by one person alone. Severalty means the owner's title is severed from any other person. Upon death of the owner, the property is transferred to the heirs or beneficiaries.

tenant
The possessor or occupant of a property.

tender
An offer by one of the parties to a contract to carry out his or her part of the contract.

tenement
Traditionally, tenement refers to real property rights which pass with the land, such as buildings and improvements; things affixed to the land. In modern times, tenement may refer to apartment buildings, especially lower-income, and run-down buildings in urban areas.

term loan
A loan for a specific period of time, usually two to ten years, repaid by regular installments, with the entire principal amount due at the end of the term.

testator/testatrix
A person who has made a will.

terminating the agreement
The process by which a buyer and seller terminate a purchase agreement. When terminating an agreement, the buyer and seller are relieved of their obligations, and all deposits are returned to the buyer, less any expenses incurred by, or on account of, the buyer up to that time.

termination of listing
The cancellation of a broker-principal contract. Most listing agreements require a specific date of termination, if a buyer is not obtained within that period. A number of other conditions exist that automatically terminate a listing agreement, including death or insanity of the principal or agent, bankruptcy of either party, condemnation or destruction of the subject property, and revocation by the principal.

termite inspection
A visual inspection of a property for the presence of termites. A licensed exterminator usually performs the inspection. Buyers may include a special condition in a sales contract that requires the sellers to provide a clean termite report.

terra cotta
Literally, "baked earth." A hard baked, glazed or unglazed ceramic material used as a decorative surface for facings and tiles.

terrazzo
Flooring made by embedding small pieces of marble or granite into cement and polishing to a high gloss.

thermal window
An insulating window or two panes of glass with air between.

thermocouple
A temperature transducer (device that converts energy) consisting of two dissimilar metals welded together at one end to form a junction that when heated will generate a voltage. The current generated in the circuit is proportional to the temperature. A thermocouple is used to measure temperature accurately.

thermostat
A switch using a bi-metallic strip that reacts to changes in temperature. Thermostats are used to regulate heating and cooling systems by switching the heating/cooling on or off as the temperature changes.

third party
A person who may be affected by the terms of an agreement but who is not a party to the agreement.

three-day notice to pay or quit
The initial notice given to a tenant to begin the eviction process in the event of non-payment of rent. The tenant must pay the amount owed, or vacate the property.

three I's formula
The process landlords should follow when evicting a tenant from a property. A landlord should use Interaction, Incentive, and Intimidation.

tight money
An economic situation in which the supply of money is limited, but the demand for money is high, resulting in high interest rates.

time
The duration of a loan.

timely manner
The time limit placed upon the performance of an act, as described in a contract.

time-price differential
The difference between the purchase price of a property and the higher total price the same property would cost if purchased on an installment basis. Under the Truth-in-Lending laws, lenders must disclose the time-price differential in any kind of installment contract.

timeshare
A specialized type of resort property where the owners purchase the right to occupy the space for a certain period of time during the year. Timeshares are often located at vacation destinations such as lakes, beaches or mountains.

title
Evidence of the ownership of land, publicly recorded in the county in which the property is located.

title exception
An item listed in a title insurance policy that is not covered by that policy.

title insurance
An insurance policy that protects the insured against loss or damage due to defects in the property's title.

title plant
The storage facility of a title company which holds and stores the complete title records of properties in its area.

title search
The reviewing of all the recorded transactions in the public record to discover any defects or clouds on a particular title, which may interfere with the transfer of the property.

title theory
The practice in some states of keeping the title to a mortgaged property with the lender until the loan is fully repaid. The borrower holds equitable title, or the right to use and possess the property.

topography
The various surface features of land.

tort
Damage, injury, or a wrongful act that is done willfully or as a result of negligence. However it does not involve breach of contract, for which a civil suit can be brought.

tourist house
A private home that accommodates travelers. Usually used by guests on bus or auto tours seeking to economize.

townhouse
A method of construction of individual houses with common side walls and a common roof. Also referred to as row houses.

township
An area of land, described by the U.S. Government Survey system. One township measures six mile-by-six miles and contains 36 sections, each one mile square.

Toxic Substances Control Act (TSCA)
A law passed by Congress in 1976, which allows the EPA to determine which substances are hazardous to the health of human beings or to the environment.

tract house
A house built as part of a subdivision, using the same building plan as many other homes in the subdivision, as opposed to a custom house, which is built to the specifications of the owner.

trade association

A voluntary nonprofit organization of independent and competing business units engaged in the same industry or trade, and formed to aid in the industry problems, promote its progress and enhance its service.

trade fixture

An article of personal property affixed to leased property by the tenant as a necessary part of business; it may be removed by the tenant upon termination of the lease. Depending on several factors, fixtures may become real property.

trading on equity

The practice of agreeing to purchase a property and then assigning the purchase agreement to another buyer before the sale closes. The original purchaser turns a profit by "selling the paper."

tranche

A portion of several related securities that may have different risk, reward and/or maturities.

transfer tax

A state tax imposed on the transfer of property, to be paid by the seller. The tax assists the state in acquiring reliable data on the fair market value of property in the state, in order to more accurately assess property taxes.

trap

A curved section of a sink's drainpipe that fills with water and provides a liquid seal to prevent the emission of sewage gases.

traverse window

A window popular in modern construction, having sashes which open horizontally, sliding on separate grooves past each other.

Treasury bill
A promissory note issued by the U.S. Treasury with a maturity date of less than one year after the date issued. Unlike a bond or note, a bill does not pay a semi-annual, fixed rate coupon, or interest payment.

Treasury bond
A bond issued by the U.S. Treasury with a maturity date from five to ten years after the date issued.

Treasury note
A promissory note issued by the U.S. Treasury with a maturity date from one to five years after the date issued.

triple net lease
A lease which requires the tenant to pay rent as well as part or all of the taxes, insurance, repairs, and other ownership expenses. Also known as an absolute net lease or net, net, net lease.

truss
A rigid, prefabricated framework of girders, struts, bars and other items that is used to support a roof or floor.

trust
A legal arrangement in which property or money is transferred from the grantor (trustor) to a trustee, to be held and managed by that person for the benefit of a third party, or beneficiary.

trust deed
Similar to a mortgage in which real property is given as security for a debt. However, in a deed of trust there are three parties to the instrument: the borrower, the trustee, and the lender (beneficiary). The borrower transfers the legal title for the property to the trustee who holds the property in trust as security for the payment of the debt to the lender or beneficiary. Also called a deed of trust.

trustee's deed
A deed given to a buyer of real property at a trustee's sale.

trustee's sale
The forced sale of real property by a lender to satisfy a debt. The sale is the final step in the foreclosure process.

trustee
In a deed of trust, the trustee is a neutral third party that holds bare legal title to the property.

trustee's deed
A written document prepared and signed by the trustee in a foreclosure sale. The deed transfers ownership of the foreclosed property to the successful bidder at the sale. The deed must be recorded in the county in which the property is located.

trust funds
Money received by real estate brokers or salespersons on behalf of others.

trust fund account
An account set up, generally by the broker, into which all the money involved in a real estate transaction is deposited. Also called an earnest money or escrow account.

trustor
The borrower under a deed of trust.

Truth in Lending Act (Regulation Z)
A truth-in-lending provision enacted in 1969 that requires lenders to inform borrowers about the cost of borrowing money, so that they may make informed choices from whom to borrow their money.

TSCA (Toxic Substances Control Act)
A law passed by Congress in 1976, which allows the EPA to determine which substances are hazardous to the health of human beings or to the environment.

two-step mortgage
A hybrid loan between a fixed-rate and adjustable-rate loan; a lower interest rate applies to the first five to seven years, and is then automatically adjusted once for the remainder of the loan period.

U

UCC (Uniform Commercial Code)
A comprehensive code of laws that governs commercial transactions. These laws help promote interstate commerce by making it easier to transact business in various jurisdictions. The UCC is accepted by every state except Louisiana.

unbalanced improvement
An improvement that is not the highest and best use of the land. It may be an over-improvement or an under-improvement.

underlying financing
A mortgage or deed of trust that takes precedence over subsequent liens, such as contracts for deed or mortgages on the same property.

underwriting
The process of determining a borrower's financial strength, on which the loan amount and terms are based. Also, the practice of buying a stock or bond, and then selling them to investors for a profit.

undisclosed agency
When a broker deals with a third party without notifying that party of the existing agency. If the agent signs his or her name to a contract without disclosing the agency, the agent then becomes fully liable for any breach of contract or failure to perform. So in order to avoid liability, and hold the principal responsible, the agent must disclose the agency.

undivided interest
Ownership by two or more persons, which entitles each to use the entire property.

undue influence
Using unfair advantage to reach agreement and acceptance of a contract.

unenforceable
A contract that was valid when made but either cannot be proved or will not be enforced by a court.

unfair and deceptive practices
Sales practices that do not necessarily involve deception, but are still considered illegal by the Federal Trade Commission (FTC). A sales practice is unfair if it offends public policy, is immoral, unethical, oppressive or unscrupulous, or causes injury to consumers. An example of an unfair and deceptive practice is pressuring buyers using intimidation and scare tactics.

Uniform Commercial Code (UCC)
A comprehensive code of laws that governs commercial transactions. These laws help promote interstate commerce by making it easier to transact business in various jurisdictions. The UCC is accepted by every state except Louisiana.

Uniform Residential Appraisal Report (URAR)
An appraisal report form requested by many federal agencies to ensure residential properties are appraised in a consistent manner.

Uniform Settlement Statement (USS)
The settlement form that must be prepared at the closing of title and must contain certain relevant closing information. Both buyer and seller are given copies and the lender must retain its copy for at least two years.

Uniform Standards of Professional Appraisal Practice (USPAP)
A set of standards for the ethical and competent development of appraisal reports.

unilateral contract
A one-sided contract where one party makes an obligation to perform, without receiving any promise in return from the other party. A good example is a reward offered for a lost cat. The other party is not obligated to look for the cat, but if they do, and they locate it, they must be paid the promised reward.

unilateral rescission
Legal action taken to repeal a contract by one party when the other party has breached a contract.

unit-in-place cost method
A method of calculating the cost of constructing a building by estimating the cost of each component part. The total is calculated by multiplying the construction cost per square foot by each of the components (material, labor, overhead, etc.).

unit (unitary) method of valuation
A valuation technique used with groups of property. The properties are valued as one thing or as integrated parts of the same system. Examples include railroads, public utilities, and pipeline companies. This is useful when the properties extend over several taxation or assessment districts.

unlawful detainer action
An action filed in court enabling a person to quickly, lawfully, and peaceably evict another person from land. Unlawful detainer actions are necessary because it is generally illegal for anyone other than the sheriff to evict someone. Even if a tenant is months behind on the rent, the landlord may not enter the premises and evict the tenant or remove the tenant's belongings. Nor may the landlord lock out the tenant, cut off the water or electricity, or remove outside windows or doors. Generally, the defendant has five days to file a response and a trial may be held within 20 days after that.

unrecorded contract
A written document that creates a legal relationship between parties but does not encumber any property. It is not publicly recorded.

URAR (Uniform Residential Appraisal Report)
An appraisal form requested by many federal agencies to ensure residential properties are appraised in a consistent manner.

urban renewal
A program under HUD in which older or substandard housing areas are improved and modernized, or demolished and replaced.

urbanization
The clustering of people around big city areas for work and living.

use clause
A clause in a lease designating which parties are authorized to use the property and for what purpose.

USPAP (Uniform Standards of Professional Appraisal Practice)
A set of standards for the ethical and competent development of appraisal reports.

USS (Uniform Settlement Statement)
The settlement form that must be prepared at the closing of title and must contain certain relevant closing information. Both buyer and seller are given copies and the lender must retain its copy for at least two years.

usury
Charging an interest rate greater than that allowed by law.

utility value
The usefulness of a property.

V

VA (Veterans Administration)
The federal agency that provides benefits to qualified veterans including the VA loan. The loan is guaranteed by the Veterans Administration and requires a low or no down payment from the borrower.

VA loan (Veterans Administration loan)
A government-sponsored mortgage assistance program. The loans require little or no down payment, have relatively easy qualification criteria, and a comparatively low rate of interest

vacancy factor
Usually refers to hotels and apartments. It is money lost due to vacancies and other collection losses, usually expressed as a percentage of scheduled gross income.

valet
An employee in a large hotel who receives, parks, and retrieves a guest's automobile.

valid
Legally binding.

valley
In home or building construction, the corner where two roof slopes meet.

valley roof
A roof whose exterior surface forms a concave angle so the edges are higher than the center.

valuable consideration
Something given up by each party to a contract in order to make the agreement binding.

valuation
The process of estimating value.

valuation date
The date on which the opinion of value applies. The date of appraisal is not necessarily the same as the date the report is written. Also called the date of value or date of appraisal.

value
The significance placed on a good or service, current or future.

value in exchange
The value of property in the marketplace.

value in use
The value of property, assuming it is in place and being used as intended.

valve
One of a variety of devices used to control the flow of liquid or gas in a system. Also used for regulating draft in a chimney connector.

variable costs
Operating expenses that change depending on level of occupancy. Examples are utilities and maintenance costs.

variable rate mortgage (VRM)
A mortgage where the interest rate varies according to an agreed-upon index, thus resulting in a change in the borrower's monthly payments.

variance
An exception to the zoning ordinance for a structure or use.

variance analysis
An analysis of reports, provided by software programs, which offers an explanation for variances from the budget.

vassal
In medieval times, a person who received a fief, or rights to land, from a regional lord.

vendee
The buyer under a contract of sale.

vendor
The seller under a contract of sale.

vendor's lien
A method of guaranteeing payment of a debt. A private loan, made by the seller, to the buyer. A vendor's lien does not involve a third party to finance the sale, as a normal mortgage does. The seller of a property places the vendor's lien on the property being sold. The lien remains on the title until the debt is fully repaid. If the buyer fails to repay the debt, the lien remains and becomes a cloud on the title, which will cause problems for the new owner when and if they attempt to re-sell the property.

veneer
Material of a better quality used to cover a lower quality surface to make it look better. Usually used on the exterior. For example, bricks that cover concrete or better wood over cheap wood.

vent
Any outlet for air. A pipe allowing air to flow into a drainage system.

vent system
When speaking of plumbing, a system of pipes and vents used to relieve pressure in a system or route gas or liquid from a building.

ventilation
The replacement of stale air with fresh air by circulation through a series of vents or a mechanical system, i.e. air conditioning.

venture capital
Unsecured money used for investing. Due to the risks involved, venture capital usually commands the highest rate of return for its investment.

vergeboard
A decorative board that hangs from the projecting edge of a sloping roof. Commonly used in the 15th century. Also called a bargeboard.

vested
Having an absolute right or title, without contingency. In investing, having the right to use a portion of a fund such as an individual retirement fund.

vestibule
A small entrance hall to a room or building.

Veterans Administration (VA)

The federal agency that provides benefits to qualified veterans including the VA loan. The loan is guaranteed by the Veterans Administration and requires a low or no down payment from the borrower.

Veterans Administration loan (VA loan)

A government-sponsored mortgage assistance program. The loans require little or no down payment, have relatively easy qualification criteria, and a comparatively low rate of interest.

vicarious liability

Liability that results not from an individual's personal actions, but from his or her relationship to the party creating the liable situation. For example, a broker is vicariously liable for the actions of a salesperson working under him, even though the broker did nothing personally.

villa

A one-story residence, usually built as a condominium. Villas are usually built in units of two or four and include parking and a small yard.

void

An agreement that is totally absent of legal effect.

voidable

An agreement that is valid and enforceable on its face, but may be rejected by one or more of the parties. An example is a contract entered into by a minor.

voluntary conveyance

A deed that conveys mortgaged property that is in default to the lender. An alternative to a foreclosure action. It is also called a deed in lieu of foreclosure.

voluntary lien
A lien placed on a property by the owner, such as a mortgage or a deed of trust.

VRM (Variable Rate Mortgage)
A mortgage where the interest rate varies according to an agreed-upon index, thus resulting in a change in the borrower's monthly payments.

W

wainscoting
The covering of an interior wall with wood or tiles from the floor to a point about halfway to the ceiling; the remaining portion is painted, wallpapered, or covered with another material different from the lower portion.

walk-through
The final inspection of a property just before the sale closes. The buyer can ensure the property has been vacated, has not been damaged, and the seller has not taken any fixtures included in the sale.

wall
A vertical divider of framing, sheathing, and plaster or wallboard, which is used to partition a building into rooms by surrounding certain areas.

warehousing
The process of assembling a number of mortgage loans into one package, and holding them for a period of time, prior to selling them to an investor. They are held while awaiting a lower discount.

warranty
A guarantee that certain facts are true.

warranty deed
A deed used to transfer title to property, guaranteeing that the title is clear and the grantor has the right to transfer it. Warranty deeds are no longer used in California.

washroom attendant
An employee in a large hotel who ensures the restroom facilities are clean and well-supplied.

water supply system
The collection of pipes and valves that deliver potable (drinkable) water to a building.

water table
The level of water saturation in the ground. Also, the structure that protrudes from a house and deflects rainwater.

watt
The unit used to measure rate of electricity used by electrical appliances.

weighted average technique
A method of averaging used in appraisal. When reconciling the results from different methods used to determine property value, the appraiser applies a weight to each approach to aid averaging.

weighted rate
A method of determining overall capitalization.

will
A written instrument a person creates which describes how he or she wishes to dispose of property after his or her death.

withholding
Holding back money for the payment of future taxes.

witnessed will
A will usually prepared by an attorney and signed by the maker and two witnesses.

wood rot
Damage to wood, caused by fungi.

workouts
Methods of resolving borrower financial problems and avoiding foreclosure, such as lengthening loan terms and reducing payments.

woven valley
A method of laying roofing material at the roof valley. The shingles are interwoven to provide maximum coverage and protection.

wrap-around trust deed
A method of financing in which a new junior loan is created that includes both the unpaid principal balance of the first loan and whatever new sums are loaned by the lender. Interest is charged on the overall total of the AITD, invariably at a higher rate than that charged on the included trust deeds. Also called an All-Inclusive Trust Deed (AITD).

writ of possession
A document that is executed at an eviction hearing that authorizes the sheriff's office to evict the tenant.

wrought iron
An easily-molded form of iron used for decorative railings, gates, furniture, etc. The term is loosely used to describe steel or aluminum used in the same manner.

Y

year-to-year tenancy
A tenancy that continues from one period to the next automatically, unless either party terminates it at the end of a period. Also known as periodic tenancy.

yield
The return on investment.

yield capitalization
The method used to estimate future value and return on investment by applying a capitalization rate to the net operating income.

Z

zero coupon bond
A bond that pays no coupons (interest), is sold at a deep discount, and matures to its face value over a specific period of time. It is traded at a deep discount because the bond pays no interest.

zero lot line
The construction of a building in which one side lies directly on the lot's boundary line. This is generally prohibited in many areas.

zero premium at settlement
A type of Private Mortgage Insurance recently initiated in California. Instead of paying the insurance premium up front, the borrower can finance the entire premium, making installment payments over the life of the loan, as if it were interest.

zoned system
A system of heating or air-conditioning that maintains different temperatures or conditions in different areas or zones in a house.

zoning
The regulation of land use. Zoning laws affect the use of land, lot sizes, types of structures permitted, building heights, setbacks, and density.

zoning estoppel
A rule that prohibits the government from enforcing a new downzoning ordinance. If a property owner spent considerable money on their property before the new downzoning took place, in the belief that the government approved all zoning requirements, the government may not enforce the new downzoning.

zoning ordinance
A use restriction applied to land.

zoning variance
A permission to deviate from a current zoning ordinance that allows a property to be of a different nature than that specified in the ordinance. A variance is not a change in or exception from the zoning.

Charts of Comparable Terms

Types of Estates

Freehold Estate	Less-than-freehold Estate				
Estate In Fee (Fee, Fee Simple, Estate of Inheritance)	**Leasehold Estate, Lease**				
• Indefinite duration • Freely inheritable • Freely transferable • Includes both present and future interest in title • Not necessarily "free and clear" of encumbrances	• Fixed duration • May be sold, assigned, or willed • Also called "chattel real"				
Fee simple absolute	**Fee simple defeasible**	**Periodic tenancy**	**Estate for years**	**Estate at will**	**Estate at sufferance**
Most complete form of ownership - no limitations or qualifications	Qualified by conditions which, if breached, may terminate or change the estate	"renting"	"leasing"	No written agreement between parties	Tenant remains after contract expires, against owner's wishes

Types of Less-than-freehold Estates

	Periodic tenancy (renting)	Estate for years (leasing)	Estate at will (no agreement)	Estate at sufferance (holdover tenant)
Creation	• Created with owner's consent.	• Created with owner's consent. • Must be in writing if lease is over one year in length.	• Created with consent of owner. No written agreement.	• Created with-out consent of owner. Tenant comes into possession lawfully.
Duration	• Continues for successive periods of the same amount of time (i.e. month to month) • Payment period not to exceed 30 days. • Tenancy period need not coincide with rent payment date.	•Continues for a definite period of time. Can be less than "years."	• Created under common law, instead of written agreement. • Continues for an indefinite period.	• Tenant remains after lease expires. • If landlord accepts rent, periodic tenancy is created.
Termination	• Notice to terminate required in writing by either party.	• Notice to terminate not required.	• Terminates at will without notice. (CA law requires notice by landlord.)	• Notice to terminate not required. Can become trespass.

Types of Leases (Estate for Years)

Flat, Fixed, or Straight	Tenant pays a fixed rent periodically.
Graduated lease	Tenant's rent varies up or down, according to escalator clause included in lease. Two types: **Step-up lease** – Rent increases over time. **Index lease** – Rent is tied to an index.
Percentage Lease	Rent is based on a percentage of gross receipts, combined with minimum fixed rent. Also known as a combination lease.
Gross Lease	Tenant pays fixed rent. Landlord pays expenses.
Net Lease	Tenant pays expenses such as taxes, maintenance, and insurance. **Triple net lease** –tenant pays all expenses.
Sandwich Lease	Tenant leases property to third party. Tenant continues to pay rent to landlord, but gives possession to third party. Original tenant remains lessee to landlord and becomes lessor to new tenant. Also known as a sublease.
Ground Lease	Lease of land only, sometimes secured by the improvements placed on the land by the user.

Types of Tenancy

	Tenancy in Common	Joint Tenancy	Community Property	Tenancy in Partnership
Parties	Any number of persons (can be husband and wife).	Any number of persons (can be husband and wife).	Only husband and wife.	Only partners (any number).
Division	Ownership can be divided into any number of interests equal or unequal.	Ownership interest must be equal.	Ownership interests are equal.	Ownership interests are in relation to interest in partnership.
Title	Each co-owner has a separate legal title to his undivided interest.	There is only one title to the whole property.	There is only one title but each co-owner has a separate interest.	Each co-owner's interest is owned in partnership for partnership's purpose.
Conveyance	Each co-owner's interest may be conveyed separately by its owner.	A conveyance by one of the joint tenants alone breaks the joint tenancy between his interest and the others but does not affect the constitution of the joint tenancy between the interests of any two or more other joint tenants.	Interests cannot be conveyed separately. Both co-owners must join in conveyance of real property. Either co-owner can transfer personal property (certain important exceptions).	Partners' individual interests in specific property cannot be conveyed separately. Any authorized partner can convey the whole partnership title.

Types of Tenancy (continued)

	Tenancy in Common	Joint Tenancy	Community Property	Tenancy in Partnership
Purchaser's Status	Purchaser will become a tenant in common with the other co-owners in the property.	Purchaser will become a tenant in common with the other co-owners in the property.	Purchaser cannot acquire one co-owner's interest and hold as community property with the other.	Purchaser can only acquire the whole title if he becomes a partner.
Survivorship	On co-owner's death his interest passes to his devisees under his will, or to his heirs. No right of survivorship.	On-co-owner's death, his interest ends and cannot be disposed of by will. Survivor owns the property by right of survivorship.	On co-owner's death, belongs to survivor in severalty, goes by will to descendant's devises or by succession to survivor.	On partner's death his interest in specific partnership property vests in the surviving partners. The values realized out of its liquidation is accounted for to his estate.
Successor's Status	Devisees or heirs become tenants in common.	Last survivor owns property in severalty.	If passing by will, tenancy in common between devisee and survivor results.	Devisees or heirs have no rights in specific partnership property.

Types of Housing

Type	Description	Distinction
Standard Subdivision	Each parcel less than 160 acres. For sale, lease, or financing.	Has no common areas. owner has no lien rights.
Planned Development (PD, not PUD)	Title to individual parcels.	Has common areas; or owner has lien rights.
Condominium Project	Title to unit and joint ownership in common areas.	Ownership of airspace only; land and building area are common areas.
Community Apartment Project	Right of possession to apartment and undivided interest in real estate with others.	Ownership is tenancy in common.
Stock Cooperative "Co-op"	Proprietary lease of apartment and stock in Cooperative	Ownership of personal property only.
Timeshare project	12 or more estates, of five years or longer, in residential structures. Timeshare Estate (ownership) or Timeshare Use (a license)	Recurrent exclusive use.
Limited Equity Housing Cooperative	A non-profit Stock Cooperative.	Low and moderate-income families. May be mobile home park. A form of subsidized housing with resale limitations.

Comparison of Mortgages and Trust Deeds

	Mortgage	Trust Deed
Parties	Two	Three
Borrower	Mortgagor	Trustor
Lender	Mortgagee	Beneficiary
Third Party	N/A	Trustee
Transaction	Contract	Contract and Conveyance
Evidence of Debt	Mortgage Note	Trust Note
Security Instrument	Mortgage Contract	Trust Deed
Security	Contract Promise	Bare legal title
Title	Remains with Mortgagor	"Bare" legal title transferred to trustee
Statute of Limitations	Outlaws four years from default date	Power of Sale clause never outlaws
Type of Foreclosure	Judicial normally; however, mortgage may contain a Power of Sale clause permitting non-judicial private sale.	Trustee's Sale normally; however, beneficiary has right to judicial sale.
Time Required to Foreclose	Judicial process likely two to three years	Trustee's sale – less than four months
Reinstatement Rights	Up to decree of foreclosure	At least three months (and up to five days prior to sale)
Redemption Rights	One year following sheriff's sale	Sale; special rules if by judicial sale

Types of Tenancy in Partnership

	General Partnership (informal)	Limited Partnership (formal)
Liability	Unlimited personal liability for each general partner.	General partner(s) has full personal liability. Limited partners have limited liability (limited to amount of contribution).
Contract	May be oral, written or implied.	Must be written, filed with the Secretary of State, and recorded in county where property is located.
Title	Title held in partnership name, individual names, or third party trustee's name.	Limited partners cannot use their names for partnership name.
Form	Active form of investment	Passive form of investment. Limited partners cannot participate in management.
Taxation	The entity is tax-reporting, but not tax-paying. Partners are individually assessed and must pay taxes.	Individual partners file separate returns and pay tax. Single taxation.
Survivorship	Death terminates the partnership, unless there is an agreement to the contrary. Title passes to survivor to supervise termination and turn over to partner's estate.	Death of the general partner terminates the partnership. Death of a limited partner does not terminate the partnership.

Types of Brokerages

Type	Advantages	Disadvantages
Corporation	• Limited liability • Central management • Not terminated by death	• Double taxation
General Partnership	• Single taxation • Partners control management	• Unlimited liability • Terminated by death
Limited Partnership	• Limited liability • Single taxation	• Limited partners: can't manage or control
Limited Liability Company	• Liability limited to amount of original investment of each member (including management).	• Annual fee based on gross income
Joint Venture	• Same as General Partnership. Same advantages.	• Applies to single project
Real Estate Investment Trust	• Same as corporation.	• Requires 100 or more investors

Real Estate Math

Formulas for computing types of interest:

Simple Interest:
I = PRT

> I = Interest
> P = Principal
> R = Rate
> T = Time

Add-on Interest rate:
AIR = $\dfrac{2IC}{P(n + 1)}$

> AIR = add-on interest rate
> I = number of installment payments per year
> C = total loan charge
> P = principal
> n = number of installments in the contract

Compound Interest:
Cs = Bd $(1 + i)n$

> Cs = compound sum
> Bd = beginning deposit
> i = interest rate per period
> n = number of periods

The Percentage Formula

Percent x Paid = Made

Variations:

Interest rate x Principal = interest earned
(An interest rate is a percentage of principal)

Rate of return x amount invested = profit
(A rate of return on an investment is a percentage
of the amount invested)

Tax rate x assessed value = annual tax
(A tax rate is a percentage of assessed value)

Commission rate x selling price = commission amount
(A commission rate is usually a percentage of selling price)

Percent of net profit x cost = profit amount
(A net profit is a percentage of cost)

Percent of gross profit x selling price = profit amount
(A gross profit is a percentage of selling price)

Rectangle and Square Area Calculations

Area = Length x Width

Length = Area ÷ Width

Width = Area ÷ Length

Area of a Square = Length x Width

Area of a Rectangle = Length x Width

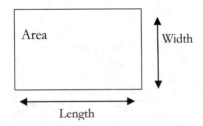

Area of a Triangle = Altitude x Base ÷ 2

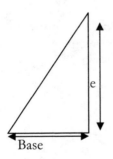

Conversion Tables

Equivalent Amounts

Percentage	Decimal	Fraction
4 1/2%	0.0045	45/1000
6 2/3%	0.0667	1/15
10%	0.10	1/10
12 1/2%	0.125	1/8
16 2/3%	0.1667	1/6
25%	0.25	1/4
33 1/3%	0.333	1/3
50%	0.50	1/2
66 2/3%	0.6667	2/3
75%	0.75	3/4
100%	1.00	1/1

U.S. Conversions

Unit	U.S. Measurement
Mile	5,280 feet; 320 rods; 1,760 yards; 80 chains
Rod	5.50 yards; 16.5 feet
Square mile	640 acres; 102,400 rods
Acre	4,840 sq. yards; 160 sq. rods; 43,560 sq. feet
Acre foot	43,560 cubic feet
Square yard	9 sq. feet
Square foot	144 sq. inches
Chain	66 feet; 100 links; 4 rods
Kilometer	0.62 mile; 3,280 feet, 10 inches
Hectare	2.47 acres

Measurement Conversions

	To convert:	To:	Multiply by:
Length	Inches	Millimeters	25.0
	Feet	Centimeters	30.00
	Yards	Meters	0.9
	Miles	Kilometers	1.6
	Millimeters	Inches	0.04
	Centimeters	Inches	0.4
	Meters	Yards	1.1
	Kilometers	Miles	0.6
Area	Square inches	Sq. centimeters	6.5
	Square feet	Sq. meters	0.09
	Square yards	Sq. meters	0.8
	Square miles	Sq. kilometers	2.6
	Acres	Hectares	0.4
	Square centimeters	Sq. inches	0.16
	Square meters	Sq. yards	1.2
	Square kilometers	Sq. yards	0.4
	Square hectares	Acres	2.5
Mass	Ounces	Grams	18.0
	Pounds	Kilograms	0.45
	Short tons	Metric tons	0.9
	Grams	Ounces	0.035
	Kilograms	Pounds	2.2
	Metric tons	Short tons	1.1
Liquid Volume	Ounces	Milliliters	30.0
	Pints	Liters	0.47
	Quarts	Liters	0.95
	Gallons	Liters	3.8
	Milliliters	Ounces	0.034
	Liters	Pints	2.1
	Liters	Quarts	1.06
	Liters	Gallons	0.26